HEREFORDSHIRE'S
HOME FRONT
IN THE
SECOND
WORLD WAR

Herefordshire's Home Front in the Second World War is a collaboration between Herefordshire Lore and Logaston Press, which was made possible by the generosity of two anonymous donors.

The book is dedicated to the memory of
Bobbie Blackwell
who did so much for Herefordshire Lore.

1946–2018

HEREFORDSHIRE'S
HOME FRONT
IN THE
SECOND
WORLD WAR

BILL LAWS

LOGASTON PRESS 🍂

FRONT COVER (*clockwise from top left*): General Post Office (GPO) Home Guard, Hereford. (*Peter Mayne*); Chelsea Pensioners at Moraston House, Bridstow. (*Gordon Armand*); Reg Robins. (*Reg Robins*); Dennis Beavan and 'Taffy' Bounds at RAF Madley. (*Dennis Beavan*); Farm workers at Court Farm, Rushall. (*Doreen Pocknell*); Nurses, with Margery Dale (*second from left*). (*Mo Burns*); Topsy Price of the Women's Land Army (WLA). (*Topsy Price*); Bob Rayner and Hazel Evans at Whitney Church. (*Tom Henderson and Jenny Hill*).

BACK COVER: Clement Attlee meeting workers at Rotherwas Munitions Factory, Hereford. (*Copyright © The Imperial War Museum*)

First published in 2019 by Logaston Press
The Holme, Church Road, Eardisley HR3 6NJ
www.logastonpress.co.uk
An imprint of Fircone Books Ltd.

ISBN 978-1-910839-33-1

Text copyright © Bill Laws, 2019

Designed and typeset by Richard Wheeler.
Cover design by Richard Wheeler.

Printed and bound in the UK by Bell & Bain Ltd., Glasgow.

Logaston Press is committed to a sustainable future for our business, our readers and our planet. The book in your hands is made from paper certified by the Forest Stewardship Council.

British Library Catalogue in Publishing Data.
A CIP catalogue record for this book is available from the British Library.

CONTENTS

Easy rider: Tom Price from Little Whitfield farm near Ross-on-Wye. He courted, and eventually married, Women's Land Army girl Nancy Price. *See page 30.* (*Nancy Price*)

ACKNOWLEDGEMENTS

All those who contributed their personal experiences to *Herefordshire's Home Front in the Second World War* are listed, with gratitude, in the people index. Special thanks are also due to Dr Elinor Kelly (elinor.kelly@smquakers.org.uk) for her exclusive research into conscientious objection in the county; to the editorial support of Logaston's Richard and Su Wheeler, and to Andy and Karen Johnson, for seeing the project off the ground; to Herefordshire Lore (Joyce Chamberlain, Sandy Green, Keith and Krystyna James, Eileen Klotz, Rosemary Lillico, Julie Orton-Davies, Harvey Payne, Chris Preece and Leominster Voices, Jean and Peter Mayne, Marsha O'Mahony, Chris and Irene Tomlinson, Linda Ward and Betty Webb); to the Rural Media Company (www.ruralmedia.co.uk) and Jo Comino for permission to use extracts from *Fieldwork*; to Herefordshire Records and Archives Centre (HARC), Herefordshire Libraries and Museum service; the Imperial War Museum; and to Gordon Armand, Maureen Beauchamp, Naomi Bell (Chilvers Cotton), Steve Binnie, Beryl Bowen, Rolly Bradstock, Elaine and Allan Brewer, Mo Burns, Geof Cole, Julie Colman, Wendy Cummins, Stasia Dzierza, Dave Edwards, Faith Ford (St James Church war memorial), Derek Foxton, Susannah Garland, Elizabeth Glover, Linda Griffin, Alan Gower, Ivan Hall, Ami Hartland, Tom Henderson, Peter Holman, Ann Johnstone, John Lambert, Gordon Lamputt, Peggy Laws, Annie Lilwall, Liz Lloyd, Louise Manning, Mandi Matthes, Anne Milne, Brian Millington, Geof Nicholls, H. Pinnell, Lita Power, Martin Prior, Eric Pugh, Peggy Putnam, Peter Redding, Winnie Reece, Tim Rowberry, Marie Standifer, Richard Taylor, Sue Taylor, June Smith, Sandra Watson, Royden Willetts, Alan Williams, Michael Young and, of course, Abby.

Herefordshire Lore works to remember, celebrate and record the county's past before it is lost with the passing of the generations. Herefordshire Lore began publishing people's memories in 1989. It works closely with Herefordshire Archive and Records Centre (HARC) and Herefordshire Libraries and Museums, and produces a quarterly magazine, *In Our Age*.

For further information, please visit: www.herefordshirelore.org.uk

FOREWORD

We all think we know lots about the Home Front during the Second World War from the TV programme *Dad's Army*, and whilst it covered lots of the topics, it did so in a light-hearted and entertaining way, not exposing the stress, danger and disruption that existed. Bill Laws, in this book, has spoken to the individuals who lived through it and has therefore used first-hand accounts, many still sharp after almost 70 years, and gives a far more realistic exposé of those turbulent times.

In the second half of the 1930s many could see another war coming; many viewed the prospect with horror, still living in the long and deep shadow of that earlier conflict which was to 'end all wars'. To many without that personal memory and with the exuberance of youth it offered an opportunity including adventure and excitement. This account illustrates all of these aspects, but especially the impact on Herefordshire, a rural county which, in many ways, time had passed by.

The impact to the county was immediate and massive. People movement went on for seven years and beyond, and saw the county's Territorial soldiers, volunteers and conscripts, both men and women, departing the county for duties at home and overseas. There was also a great influx of people: refugees, evacuees, workers and servicemen and -women. In addition to British forces, there were those from overseas (especially Polish and, later in the war, Americans and Canadians). Herefordshire was far from the possible invasion beaches and thus became part of the secure home base, with training units (RAF Madley, Credenhill and Shobdon), factories and depots at Rotherwas, Pontrilas, Moreton-on-Lugg and many smaller establishments throughout the county; troop concentration areas at Foxley, Barons Cross, Hereford Racecourse, Berrington Hall and Eastnor Park to name a few. Schools, convalescence hospitals and even the old soldiers from the Chelsea hospital were evacuated to Herefordshire. The locals generally welcomed these newcomers and also fully supported the county's war effort. My grandfather from Ledbury was employed at ROF Rotherwas, and Fred Raper, killed in the explosion, was a family acquaintance (*see page 95*).

The invasion threat was real and 'Dad's Army' was a real force. Many members had seen action in the First World War. Their objective was to hold up any invading forces to buy time for Regular troops to be organised to defeat the invasion. They knew what this meant and accepted it. They were seen as such an important element of the UK's defence that the Home Guard often received equipment before it was issued to the Regular Army; this included the Thompson machine gun. They were not the joke portrayed in *Dad's Army*, but there were of course lighter moments. When the Home Guard was stood down on December 1944 there were over 7,000 men in the six Battalions of the Herefordshire Home Guard. There were units in almost every village and town, as well as factory units at Rotherwas and Barronia Metals, and a Great Western Railway unit as well. Perhaps as many as 25% of eligible men had served in the Home Guard (including my Father in Ledbury until called up for RN service). In addition there were Air Raid Wardens, Fire and Rescue Squads, Auxiliary policemen, Nurses, WRVS, Salvation Army, WI and many other welfare institutions.

It can clearly be seen that the whole of British society and the economy were geared to support the war effort. The war touched everyone; times were tough even after the years of the depression, but there was a determination and camaraderie born from shared hardships and a common purpose. There was opportunity for adventure and humour but there was the ever present 'black cloud' and threat of bad news. Bill shows these highs and lows of life in Herefordshire during World War Two: it is a valuable record based on individual experiences.

Colonel Andy Taylor OBE DL

Andy Taylor was born and educated in Ledbury, where his family had lived for at least three generations. He joined the Army in 1977 and was Commissioned from the Royal Military Academy Sandhurst and served for the next 32 years in various parts of the world. He retired back to Herefordshire in 2009. He is curator of The Herefordshire Light Infantry Museum and has been researching the history of the regiment for over 30 years. He is currently The Rifles County Colonel for Herefordshire.

ı | We All Grew Up that Night

WHEN VICTORY IN EUROPE (VE) DAY DAWNED ON MONDAY 8 MAY 1945 PEOPLE threw caution to the winds and celebrated wherever they were. While one party settled down to a ration-free tea in the middle of Hereford's Church Street, prisoner of war Jack Hill, having been abandoned by his German guards, sought out and found some American GIs: 'What a welcome we received.'

Ted Woodruff, meanwhile, was sitting on the banks of the Rhine with his army mates surveying the wastelands of what had been the industrial Ruhr. 'The war in Europe was over. We broke out the rum rations.' Student teacher Barbara Sharpe stood by the Hereford College bonfire, singing songs and baking potatoes; munitions worker Beryl Sadler tripped into High Town on a pair of home-made high-heeled shoes; and Royal Navy man Jim Lawes was caught up in a conga through central London, dancing down the Mall to Buckingham Palace.

Many of Jim's shipmates were still at war. Chief Petty Officer G. Short, a gunnery instructor on board the aircraft carrier HMS *Victorious*, had abandoned his VE Day celebrations as Japanese kamikaze pilots attacked their ship, steaming towards Taiwan. One bomber crashed into the flight deck killing three crew.

The war in Asia had another three months to run, but when news came through of the Japanese surrender following the dropping of the atomic bombs on Hiroshima and Nagasaki, Hereford student teacher Gladys Pugh was in Cheltenham with a group of other students: 'We all grew up that night,' she recalled.

The Second World War had a devastating effect on Herefordshire and its people. Britain had declared war on Germany on 3 September 1939, 21 years after the First World War, which killed over 3,000 of its citizens and wounded thousands more. People in Herefordshire looked on the approach of this second war with deep misgivings: 'You'd been brought up not long after the 1914–1918 war, so it was very much to the front of your mind,' remembered Air Force man Jim Thomas.

OPPOSITE: a victory march through Hereford High Town in 1945. Behind the band, Squadron Leader Gordon Lamputt leads the Hereford Air Training Corps. (*Gordon Lamputt*)

In fact, local casualties would be less than half those in 1914–18, despite the war lasting two years longer in Europe, and three years longer in the Far East. The Second World War would also herald significant social change. Just as the first war introduced a state pension, improved women's rights and saw the closure of the detested workhouses, the second war signalled a boom in social housing and a free national health service. No longer would families have to suffer the experience of this Hereford mother, her husband away fighting in Italy in 1944: 'I called the doctor out to my daughter because she was sick. "I can't come out to charity cases," he says. When he does come out to see her, she was dead.'

The global war was waged between two great military alliances: the Allies (France, Poland, the United Kingdom and its territories including India, Australia, New Zealand, Canada, South Africa, the Netherlands, Belgium, Greece and Yugoslavia and, after Pearl Harbour, America); and the Axis (Germany, Italy and the Soviet Union, which then changed to the Allies' side in 1941, and Japan, already at war with China). The war would be marked by genocide, massacres, the aerial bombing of civilians and the first use of nuclear weapons. War played out across the world, from the wintery wastes of Archangel in northern Russia to Japanese death camps in the Burmese jungle; from sunny shipyards on America's west coast to olive-covered foothills at Monte Cassino in Italy; and from the gritty deserts surrounding Tobruk in North Africa to the muddy shores of the Lower Rhine at Arnhem. In each and every one of these theatres of war there would be a Herefordshire man or woman serving their country.

When finally the men were demobbed and the women quit their wartime posts to make way for them, everyone settled to rebuild wounded lives in a nation crippled by seven years of conflict. Over the next 75 years these erstwhile soldiers, sailors, airmen, postmen, police officers, internees, prisoners of war, land girls, timber Jills, firemen, Home Guardsmen, teachers, evacuees and munitioneers would reflect on how the war had affected them. In letters, interviews and latterly by email, combatants, service people and their children have shared their experiences with the county reminiscence group, Herefordshire Lore. Many recollections have been published in its journals; others are revealed here for the first time.

This, then, is their testimony. However it is only the start of our efforts to record more memories of what may prove to have been the worst event of the twentieth century.

2 On the Home Front

Schoolgirl Jeanette Reed was playing outside her Stonebow Road home in Hereford on 3 September 1939. 'I was wearing my green dress,' she recalled. 'But when I went inside my mother was standing at the top of the stairs, crying. "What's the matter?" I asked her. "War just broke out," she said.' Jeanette's father had already served in one world war. He was about to enlist in his second.

The British Prime Minister Neville Chamberlain made his announcement – 'This country is at war with Germany' – at 11.15 a.m. People across Herefordshire received the news with both sadness and resignation. One young teacher, newly qualified from Hereford's training college, was waiting for her train at Ross Station, excited at the prospects of the new life that lay ahead of her. She had secured a teaching post at Grove Lane Infant's School in Birmingham, and a bed at the city's Young Women's Christian Association (the YWCA). Suddenly, a porter dashed down the platform. 'Germany's attacked Poland. We're at war,' he shouted. She continued her journey, admitting later: 'Our hearts sank.'

Fifteen-year-old Jim Thomas lived with his family in Foley Street, Hereford. The news did not surprise him: he knew war was coming. 'People thought in the late 1930s there was going to be another war. We could sense it.' His father, a driver with Midland Red buses, would be too old for the armed forces, but the teenager knew it was now his turn to enlist: 'I wanted to go into the Air Force and that was it.'

Declaration of war: when Prime Minister Neville Chamberlain announced, 'This country is at war with Germany', schoolgirl Jeanette Reed (later Jeanette Bates) found her mum in tears at the family home in Stonebow Road. Jeanette's father Arthur Reed (*above right*) had already fought in one world war. He was about to go to war again. (*Jeanette Bates*)

3

Elizabeth Newall, another student-teacher at Hereford College, knew war was unavoidable and she guessed, rightly, it would be like no other war that had gone before. 'It was obvious that the war, seemingly inevitable after 1938, would be vastly different from its predecessor. Above all, the development of air striking power during the intervening 20 years meant that civilians would be in the front line.'

Many Herefordshire people would experience being bombed from above. The British air raids that devastated German cities such as Dresden were widely condemned in the years after the war. The response, that the German Luftwaffe had started it, was not without foundation. Herefordshire's industrial neighbours suffered heavy and repeated air raids from the 1940s, and the sound of the German bombers lumbering overhead frightened many people. Others found themselves directly caught up in the bombings.

Joan Laurie (then Joan Davies) was running Joan's Baby Shop in Commercial Road. 'I was in the draper's trade at Kings and Son when the shop came up. Mother was widowed so we ran it together.' Their supplier was Mr Holmes of Peel Watson in Manchester, and she paid for the goods in person:

War threatens: the war brought Jim Thomas and Joan Hammond together. Fifteen years old when war was declared, Jim joined the RAF as soon as he was old enough. Joan, meanwhile, left her home in Shropshire having signed up with the Women's Timber Corps. They met in Hereford and married in November 1947. (*Joan Thomas*)

> I'd catch the 2.30 a.m. train to Manchester with butter and eggs from my sister's farm and all the cash in my bag. You'd be dodging the bombs to get to the warehouse. Then I'd give Mr Holmes the butter and eggs, pay for the order and be back on the Hereford train for 6.00 p.m.

In 1940 the warehouse was destroyed and 400 people were killed.

Edith Gammage was living with her husband Horace and new baby at Brislington in Bristol. 'We were just off the Bath Road, quite a nice area, not very far from Filton aerodrome.' Horace was working as a laundry engineer on military uniforms. One day Edith was startled by an air raid. 'There was no warning. I heard a terrific noise: "God, that sounds like bombing and screeching." It was a big raid on Filton aerodrome, about twelve o'clock in pure daylight. It killed a terrific amount of people.' (RAF Filton was bombed on 25 September 1940, with over 200 people dying when one of the shelters received a direct hit).

The raids continued. 'We were badly bombed [and] it was awful. We were either downstairs under the stairs or out in the shelter – I didn't feel safe sleeping in bed.' The Gammage's shelter was deep underground. 'I'd got an old single bedstead from a scrap merchant's and a mattress so that was pretty comfortable to sleep on. The bedside table was an old orange box turned upside down.' Despite these home comforts, Edith felt close to panic in the shelter:

> There was a big Catholic place that used to come around with great big churns [of water] so we had enough for each day (although not when you got washing to do). But I couldn't stand having to go into the shelter. It was cold and the power was usually gone. Horace would start a little fire and put on a saucepan for the baby's feed.

Finally, when a time-bomb fell in their back garden and blew out the house windows, Edith's spirit snapped. 'That was it. We came home to my mother's in Tupsley and within a fortnight Horace was called up.'

Jim Thomas again: 'It was difficult to put things into perspective because you started talking about loyalty and patriotism. You'd been brought up not long after the most horrible, terrible war that has probably ever been.' Like so many others in Herefordshire, his family had suffered casualties. 'My mother had lost two brothers and her fiancé in that war, so it was very much to the front of their minds.' He reflected on how people marked the anniversaries of the First World War:

> Events like Armistice Day were rigidly observed, especially the two-minute silence. At St Owen's School we would assemble in the hall and the senior master – usually Mr Webber – would read the Roll of Honour. I couldn't understand why tears ran down his face. After this war I could.

Michael Young, then only five, recalled a sobering walk from the family home in Barrs Court. 'After Neville Chamberlain's broadcast had finished, Dad and I walked to his parents at 14 College Green.' There were other family members present, but the atmosphere was tense, discussions subdued. 'There were no cheery greetings. Uncles George and Bob, who had both been wounded in the last war, must have had their own thoughts to contend with.' A few weeks later Michael's Dad arrived home unexpectedly: 'It was unknown for my father to appear at home on a weekday at mid-morning and my mother, busy at her ironing, uttered the one word: "Why?" There was tension in the air.' His father, then around 28, had been for his medical, prior to being called up. 'It wasn't until many years later that I realised the significance of these events.'

The declaration of war did not surprise Betty Griffiths. Engaged to be married, she was living with her family at Rotherwas near the Royal Ordnance Factory where her father worked. Their home overlooked the works that had started producing munitions during the First World War. In 1918 the factory had been mothballed, but now there were signs that it was being prepared for action. 'There was war in the air, you know, and the factory was getting primed ready for it. You could sense it.' As tensions grew in Europe the War Office began moving explosives onto the site:

> It must have been 1938, we used to get these four young fellows in their early-20s bringing powder [in] these big container vans down from Stockton-on-Tees to the factory. We called them the Powder Boys. They were never bothered that they were carrying dangerous stuff. They'd be on overnight stay to get it unloaded. Mother always put them up.

Wilf Bowen was one of the supervisors at Rotherwas: 'The factory had ticked over between the wars and now they were busy putting on as many staff as they could get up, because they obviously knew what was coming off. They were busy re-arming.'

Despite these preparations, many feared that Britain would soon be overrun by the Germans. Eileen Carpenter, a Birmingham evacuee, recalled how most people, following the fall of Belgium, and of Paris in June 1940, 'thought war would be over by Christmas.'

The prospect of the Town Hall Union Jack being pulled down and replaced with the sinister black and red swastika of the Third Reich seemed inevitable to this group of student teachers studying at Hereford College. 'All of us thought the Germans would soon arrive,' recalled Vera Bengry (then Vera Wardman): 'We decided all dark-haired [girls] would not survive.'

This sense of resignation, and the expectation that Britain, like France, Belgium and Poland, would soon become an outpost of the new German empire, was countered by a feeling of excitement, especially amongst the young. There was a touch of glamour to the idea of fighting for freedom, of defending the country against Hitler and the 'Hun'. Jim Thomas looked forward to reaching his 18th birthday and joining the RAF: 'I wouldn't say that, for my age, this was the worst possible time.' Some young people were frustrated when they felt themselves being denied a piece of the action – or at least the chance to don a uniform. Kathleen Jones lived with her father, mother and brother at the firemen's quarters in Rotherwas. All the family, except for Kathleen, worked on the munitions. While she longed to join the forces, Kathleen instead found herself marooned in a hair-dressers' shop, W.R. Jones & Son in West Street, Hereford. The proprietors were too frail to run the shop, and since their son had left to serve in the RAF, Kathleen was appointed to manage the business. All hopes of a glorious military service were fading rapidly. 'I got deferred from going in the forces and [yet] I wanted some excitement.' She finally donned a uniform after joining the Girls Training Corps on Hereford's College Estate, her humdrum days coming to a halt when she was caught up in the aftermath of the

Girls from the Ministry: the war created work for everyone, including these young women at the Ministry of Agriculture and Fisheries Feeding Stuff, pictured by the Castle Pool, Hereford surrounding their boss, John Thompson. Ivy Manning (née Billings) (*second left, back row*) recalled some of the other names including Joan Jones, Joan Lloyd, Pamela Popplestone, Violet Priday, Josie Vanstone and 16-year-old Gwen Thomas (*front left*) who died suddenly of tuberculosis. (*Ivy Manning*)

huge explosion which rocked the factory in May 1944 (*see 'On the Munitions', page 85*). 'Dad was driving the fire engine down [at the factory]. Our house was a bit of a shambles afterwards, glass on the beds and all that, so I had to stay with an aunt in Park Street while my brother stayed with another aunt in Edgar Street.'

As the war progressed, people were forced to become more flexible in their family arrangements. Children were sent to live with distant friends or family members to keep them out of harm's way and, sometimes, to help out with some extra labour. Pam Bengry's family moved from London to Eardisland when the Blitz began. In an interview she described seeing distressing scenes when little children, evacuated from their own city homes, were dispatched to new ones in Herefordshire. 'These young children were just held up with someone shouting: "Who would like this one?" The children didn't seem to be crying. They were quiet, shocked, I think.'

Brummie Eileen Carpenter had been sent to live with a family acquaintance:

> Our family happened to be on holiday in Hereford when war was declared. We had been packed and ready to leave on the train, but my parents, concerned that Birmingham would be bombed, decided to leave me with this "aunt" – I called her aunty but you called everyone aunty or uncle in those days. (*See 'Evacuees', page 71*)

Little Rosemary Lillico, only two years old when war was declared, lived with her extended family in a big house on Penn Grove Road, Hereford. Her grandparents, mother, two married aunts and their husbands, and three uncles mucked in together. Three of the men were in the army while her grandfather, one uncle and her aunt Rose worked at Painter Brothers. Rose later found work at the munitions factory. As the war moved on, five of the family left with Rosemary to live in a farm cottage at Breinton, leaving aunty Rose, still unmarried but now with a new baby, back in Hereford.

Life was tough. 'Mum and Dad were expected to work on the land – and, of course, we children went with them to pull mangles and sugar beet on freezing cold mornings, planting potatoes, picking apples and helping out when the wheat, oats and barley were harvested.' Her dad's generous garden kept the family in vegetables, and chickens, ducks and the pigs provided extra rations.

Rosemary was allowed to spend occasional weekends back at Penn Grove Road with her aunt Rose. 'I'd wait until she came home from work at Rotherwas – she smelled awful from the munitions so the first thing was a bath and a hair wash with Dinkie curlers put in her hair.' Rosemary enjoyed watching Rose get ready for a night out dancing, dressing in her best clothes and putting gravy browning on her legs to make believe she wore stockings:

> She would stand on a chair while my aunty or grandpa put a line up the back of her legs with eyebrow pencil. Sometimes with a wink she would say to me: "If I play my cards right you might have some gum in the morning." I didn't quite understand.

Not until she was eight did Rosemary discover her 'aunt' Rose was in fact her mother.

War demanded feverish economic activity, and the revitalised munitions factory, the construction of new RAF bases and military camps, such as Foxley, meant work for everyone in a rapidly changing social scene. Or almost everyone – Marie Wills (later Marie Hill), a girl at the inner city Catholic school, wondered why two of her school friends had stopped attending. The girls were Italian and their parents ran a fish and chip shop in High Town. 'I don't know whether their parents were taken because they were foreigners, but if you were Italian or whatever, you were sent off to somewhere else.'

In 1939, the principal of the teachers' college on College Hill, Miss Jennings, was in the process of moving her institution to Goodrich Court in the south of the county. She was making way for the Ministry of Agriculture and the Scottish Office, which had commandeered the College. The order was rescinded shortly before the start of term, and college staff instead toiled through September cutting up bales of Italian cloth to blackout the building's 428 windows. A newly recruited lecturer, Miss Mycock, recalled:

OPPOSITE Full employment: Beryl Farr from College Road went to work at the Hereford telephone exchange after a spell at the Rotherwas munitions factory. (*Beryl Taylor*)

Crane drivers: as employees – like these men from Painter Brothers – left to join the forces, the women stepped up to take their places. They included sisters Ruby Fox and Nancy Hooper who became crane drivers at Painter Brothers. (*Nancy Hooper*)

'The days were curiously similar. We rose, breakfasted, blacked-out, lunched, blacked-out, drank tea, blacked-out, gathered for supper (...) and afterwards gathered in Miss Jennings' drawing room to hear the news and knit comforts for the troops.'

The College cellars, now equipped with bunk beds, were reinforced to serve as air raid shelters, and College teams of firewatchers, one staff member to three students, were recruited. A sub-warden's post was set up and students received first aid and fire-fighting demonstrations before being formed into squads of fire-fighters. Their role was to assist with such emergencies as a plane crash, a bombing raid or a gas attack. Mustard gas had been developed and stored at the munitions factory during the First World War and it was widely believed that poison gas would become a weapon of choice during these hostilities. Everyone was issued with a gas mask and the College garage was turned into a gas 'cleansing station' where enthusiastic boys were recruited from the surrounding College Estate to volunteer as gas casualties during exercises.

A day nursery was opened at the College in 1942, and run by former student Miss G. Meredith to help mothers, like Rosemary's mum Rose, who were now making munitions at Rotherwas (another crèche was based in the Cathedral precinct by the Bishop's Palace). The Women's Voluntary Service also based a local Housewives Service Scheme

More munitions: there were regular appeals to help fund the war. (*Keith James*)

at the College. The housewives gave demonstrations to their neighbours on how to smother incendiary bombs with sand mats, or toured the town collecting money for the Red Cross Penny-a-Week Fund and War Weapons Weeks.

Through the young eyes of Frances Wilson, just starting at St James School in Bartonsham the year before, life under headmistress Miss Hall seemed normal enough. She learned to write and read, knitted dishcloths (the boys made raffia mats), helped with the class garden and enjoyed her daily milk ration. There was maypole dancing accompanied on the school piano (Frances' father tuned pianos at Gilbert and Leslie Heins' music shop on Broad Street) and country dancing on the Castle Green. But when the air raid sirens sounded the children were trained to race to particular houses – the ones with cellars. 'My mother once found my sister out in the street as no one was home at her allotted house.' Eventually they were allowed to share the underground shelters at the General Hospital nearby: 'When the sirens sounded we were escorted through the vicarage grounds with our gas masks and torches to the Hospital shelters' (Joan Clark recalled how even babies had gas masks).

Herefordshire now looked like a county at war. Jim Thomas watched men with oxy-acetylene cutters remove the metal gates and railings from outside his Foley Street home (they were to be melted down for munitions), while wooden gates and metal tube railings were installed in their place.

There were swathes of khaki in the shops, military vehicles in the streets and armed guards at every strategic corner. Military personnel assembled for official photographs. Doris Townsend, who had recently been rejected for a job at the Post Office because she was left-handed, had started working for Ada Durrant, the proprietor of Vivian's photographers in High Town. For her wage of 2/6d a week Doris took and printed photographs, retouched negatives and often accompanied Miss Durrant on her regular commissions to take military group photographs. She and Ada, along with Ada's beloved cocker spaniel, Timmy Baba, would be chauffeured by a Mr Weaver from Marriotts Garage to Bradbury Lines, Credenhill, Shobdon and Merebrook Camp near Malvern. On one journey to Merebrook, Doris had confided to Ada about a discreet relationship she was enjoying with a second lieutenant there (husband-to-be Cyril Kershaw). Doris broke out in blushes when her employer swept into the mess proclaiming, 'Sit down men: I know Second Lieutenant Kershaw.'

Finding one's way around required good local knowledge as most village signposts had been removed to confuse enemy agents. Men in reserved occupations, meanwhile, were receiving secret training in guerrilla warfare. 'We had four or five units [in Herefordshire], each with a secret operational base,' recalled one county landowner. 'The idea was to disrupt Jerry [and] if possible to kill an officer.' (*See 'Subterfuge and Deception', page 133*).

Heavy gear: in 1940 a labour crew prepare Shobdon's airfield for active service with their D8 Caterpillar and trailer. The crew (*from left to right*): Jim Mifflin (Pembridge), George (Merthyr), Phil (Leicester), 'Little John' (Cholstrey), John Yates (Pembridge), Charlie Conod (Barrons Cross) and Jimmy Jones from Leominster on the tractor. Jim Mifflin's son Noel recalled visiting the site at weekends for a ride on the tractor: 'George and Phil travelled with the contractors while the local men stayed on the airfield. John Yates was called up later and served in the army, returning safely at the end of hostilities.' (*Noel Mifflin*)

Young Henry Moss from Aconbury found himself involved in a different kind of clandestine affair. His stepfather George Bywater was employed by farmer Arnold Layton of Aconbury Court:

> One summer's evening Mr Layton asked me to take the chalice and collection plate for safe-keeping in a bag through the woods to Mr Payne at Merrivale Farm, which was a long way for my little legs. The farmer was going to block off half the cellar to store local valuables until after the war. The German invasion was expected at any time and it was felt that any valuables seized by the Germans would be sent out of this country and back to Germany.

Henry's reward for saving the church plate was some biscuits from Mr Payne and a pocket full of silver paper he picked up on the way home. He decided it had been dropped by German planes in an effort to distort radar. 'We later used it to make Christmas decorations – we didn't waste anything in those hard times.'

Dance your cares away: wartime saw an upsurge in village dances and dance bands like the local, US-influenced 'The Rhythmists'. Seated centre is Col F.J. McDonald, commanding the U.S. 123rd Medical Company and there to welcome the Allied Entertainments Committee's Concert Party to his hospital at Foxley. Historian Derek Foxton has identified the line up as: (*left to right, standing*) Miss Fecht, Miss Joseph, B. Nicholas, K. Barwick, Wynne Oxlade, and 'The Rhythmists' with Mr Cross [compère], Daphne Slim, Miss Schieber, and Miss D. Turner. Front (*kneeling*): Dorothy Turner's Juveniles. Daphne Slim performed the classic *Don't Fence Me In* during the performance, while Frank Slater went on to be resident organist at the Ritz in Commercial Road, Hereford for many years. (*Maureen Beauchamp/ Derek Foxton*)

Henry had recently mastered his bicycle, and used to ride the two miles from his Aconbury home to school in Little Dewchurch. One morning his teacher, Miss Fuller from Little Birch, asked the children to bring in all spare pots, pans and frying pans for the war effort. 'Following this, one day en route to school, a brand new Spitfire flew over. I thought, "that's our frying pan in that one!"'

Country people were accustomed to finding their way in the dark, but city people found it harder to manage without street lights. Joan Clark lived in the confines of a small house on Park Street, Hereford with her mother, father, sister and an evacuee ('she'd be about eighteen and she was working – it was compulsory to have her.') Their home, like everyone else's, had to be fully blacked out – 'every window: you dare not shine a light, and you'd think twice about going anywhere in the dark. One night the sirens went and we all had to go down the cellars – they got cellars in the old houses in Park Street – with our gas masks.'

The combination of the blackout and the arrival of black American soldiers prior to the invasion of France and the D-Day landings brought its own complications. Katie Causer recalled how Hereford racecourse was tented right through the war: 'All nationalities were there, but the black and white Americans were strictly separated – the blacks were on the Roman Road side; the whites on the Grandstand Road side and the two sides could never cross. I don't think the black GIs were even allowed into the local dances.' One young mother, Katy Deem, left her friend's house on the College estate late one night:

> It was twelve o'clock. I said to my friend: "You got to get up for work and I got to walk all the way home."
> "Cheerio," she said. I turns round and I hear "thump, thump, thump". There was no lights or anything. I couldn't see nothing. And all of a sudden I saw teeth!

She had stumbled into a black GI as they crossed the railway bridge. 'I stopped and he looked at me and said: "Can I take you home, Missy?"'

She gave him short shrift: 'I said: "Look son," I said, "I got children older than you", I said, "and I've also got a husband at home waiting for me. Good night!" I turned on me heels.' She heard no more and had no cause to use her secret weapon: 'I never went out at night without an umbrella. I used to think: "I'll poke him in the middle!"'

As war went on people learned to cope with increasingly difficult circumstances. One thing that proved a constant problem was food.

3   Food, Farm and Field

I N THE THIRTIES, FOLLOWING THE WORLDWIDE ECONOMIC DEPRESSION, LIFE FOR most country people was hard, but productive. All that was about to change.

John Barnet was born at Stretton Grandison in the early 1930s, and moved with his mother and father into his grandmother's black and white thatched cottage, the Bean Field at Woodsend, in around 1938. 'The cottage was nice inside. The only thing was the bath was in the kitchen, a proper bath with a top on it. We had a toilet outside but he was a flush toilet: there wasn't many that had them.' His father, born in 1905, registered for active service, but was too old to go. Instead he worked the winters wiring in the hop yards, and the rest of the year as a cattle man with H.R. Griffiths' pedigree herd of Hereford cattle at Little Tarrington.

John remembered the first sign of enemy action:

> This bomb came down towards Canon Frome after we'd got to bed. A 'whistler' it was called: it never went off. Made a hell of a noise but no bang. And another one dropped at Alders End, Tarrington, not far from where my father was working on the hop wires. They weren't allowed in the hop yard the next day, and when the bomb was dug out they found it was full of sand.

The theory was that resistance workers in a German munitions factory had sabotaged the bomb.

Still a child, John was nevertheless required to manage his own vegetable plot on the Griffiths' farm:

> I'd be seven or eight and father taught me. He had two bigger patches, [each] about 20 yards by 15. We was expected to help in the garden and I was encouraged to grow all sorts – lettuce, radish, perhaps a row of peas. Father used to grow his parsnips, shallots, onions and carrot seed and then we bought our [other] seeds from Woolworths in Ledbury.

Bread and bombs: Geof Nicholls' father ploughing at Netherton Farm on Eastnor Estate near Ledbury. County farms had a critical role in the war, especially when Axis forces began sinking merchant ships bringing supplies to Britain. (*Geof Nicholls*)

Dig for Victory: Naomi Edwards and her brother help dig up the vegetable patch at the back of the family home, 30 Cotterell Street, Hereford for an Anderson air raid shelter. (*Dave Edwards*)

Like most country people they kept a few fowl and often went rabbiting with their ferret:

> I always took the dog, a little rough, white, long-haired terrier given me by a Gypsy (I'd watered his horse when he was up in the meadow next to us and he gave me a dog for doing it). If you took the dog to a rabbit hole and he held his foot up, there was a rabbit there. Then you put nets on the holes, put the ferret in and with luck the rabbit comes out into the net.

Cutting down on hops: Beryl Bowen, (*right, on her mother's lap*), at Weston Beggard hop yard in the 1930s. The war saw hop production cut back to allow Herefordshire farmers to produce more home-grown wheat. (*Beryl Bowen*)

Self-sufficiency was as much a necessity as a virtue. Having no fridge or freezer to store the meat they would 'pull the neck' of no more than two rabbits at a time. Those were expected to last a couple of days. 'We'd paunch them – take the insides out – and bury that, [give] the liver to the ferret as a sort of reward.' John's favourite dish was roast rabbit with stuffing: 'Mum made the stuffing; you didn't buy anything.'

Phyllis Yapp returned home to stay with her family who ran the Builders Arms at Bearwood near Pembridge after her husband was called up:

> You saved everything in those days. We used to catch rabbits, have two rabbits hanging up on the back door, one for stew and one for roast. Mum used to make lard. Used to buy it from Higg's the butchers, put it in the saucepan and heat it. She used to have a sieve and let it drain through, you know? It was pure white. I used to make the pastry with that. It was lovely. I used to make a bit of butter, take the cream off the milk, [leave it a] couple of days, put it in a jar

then put a lid on it and shake it, separate it, take the lid of the jar off, and the whey that was left, made the cakes with it. Even though it was the war time we done very well really.

City life was very different. Margery Dale (later Burman) recalled men from Birmingham coming to Hereford to escape the Blitz and buy food: 'They came down every weekend. The men came to fish on the Wye and get some sleep. And they came to us for eggs, butter, anything we could let them have.' On one occasion Margery went outside to watch an airplane passing overhead: 'One of the Birmingham men called me in. "Don't go outside; they're very handy with their rear gunners."' Margery also remembered how the men hunkered down on the river bank and caught up with their lost sleep in the open air. Later in the war Margery served as a nurse: 'The food wasn't bad considering it was war time. We had a meeting once [about conditions for nurses] and we said we didn't want any more money – all we wanted was slightly better food.'

Bacon, butter and sugar were first rationed in January 1940. Gradually, fish, tea, milk, eggs, cheese and a host of other groceries were added to a list which continued in force until 1954. Rationing applied to everyone and, although it impacted on towns-people more, their country cousins were also affected. 'You had to use your ration cards,' recalled John Barnett who was partial to rationed dried egg powder. 'I don't think there were any eggs anywhere near it, but it made bloody good scrambled egg.' Teenager Betty Webb (*see 'Evacuees', page 71*), then living in London, found a £1.5s-a-week job keeping the books in the St Johns office of an East End meat processing company owned by Montague Gluckstein Abrahams. 'Every pie, every piece of that ghastly luncheon meat, had to be accounted for. The salesmen would bring in these greasy little bits of paper and, because of rationing and the black market, everything had to be weighed out.' Nevertheless, Betty enjoyed her work: 'I loved it, adding up all the pounds and ounces, and pounds, shillings and pence.'

Student teacher Pat Ord (formerly Pat Jones) made a note of her fellow students' wartime rations in a college record book: 'Outside the dining room stood lockers for our rations. Each week the dining hall reps weighed out 2oz margarine, 2oz butter and 4oz of sugar for each student. Once a month we had a jar of either jam or marmalade.'

The rationing of cooking fat was a perennial problem. Still a child during the war, Aileen Hepworth and her four older sisters were constantly reminded by their mother to 'scrape it on, scrape it off, because you could only put it very thinly on your bread.' Despite rationing, Aileen's family never went hungry. 'My dad had two allotments so he grew all the vegetables. You took your own jug to the dairy for the milk and my mother used to get the curds and use it in cheesecake – curd tart.' If she could save enough fat to make a pastry case she would beat an egg into the curds, stir in some sultanas and, flavouring it with nutmeg, bake it in the oven.

Aileen recalled her mother's many other economies, which included ordering her bacon thin cut ('number 9'), using suet for puddings and buying cows' hearts because 'the beasts' hearts were big. She'd buy one and she'd roast it, and that lasted quite a few days, sliced up, with some gravy. It was good nourishing food.'

Hedgerow fruit was picked and bottled when in season and, on one momentous occasion, Aileen's mother procured a couple of oranges. 'Wonderful! By now two of my sisters were working and, I don't know how it happened, but they started fighting over these oranges.' One of the sisters' boyfriends, Billy, was dispatched to break up the battle.

Finding food for the table was not the only problem people encountered.

> When my second eldest sister got married they had great difficulty finding fruit for the wedding cake. And then there was the clothing ration: everything was mended, darned, then passed down. I'd never got any new clothes, because I had four older sisters and their old clothes all came down to me.

Student teacher Pat Ord recalled meals at Hereford College. After grace ('a two-part *Non Nobis*') had been sung, the midday meal was served. 'We sat at long refectory tables and were served from an enormous dish at the end. We dreaded fish, complete with heads and eyes, served in a white sauce and known as "whale and whitewash."'

Fish proved unpopular in other quarters. Tupsley's Brian Davies had been living in Cardiff when he enlisted in the RAF. He was destined to become a fighter pilot (*see 'The War Above', page 97*). After going by train from Cardiff to London, he and hundreds of other recruits gathered at

Tough times: with everything from dried fruit and icing sugar to clothing and petrol in short supply, wartime weddings were performed on a shoestring. (*Alan Gower*)

Lord's Cricket Ground and sat waiting without food or drink. Finally they were marched to Paddington and put on a train to Torquay. 'We spent the whole day with nothing to eat until we reached Babbacombe where I had my first meal with the RAF: great mugs of cocoa and thick bread layered with margarine.' Brian developed a taste for the RAF's kidney dish, stewed in thick gravy on fried bread ('it went down in about three gulps'), but he never came to terms with the locally caught whiting. A meal of whiting, he said, was like trying to eat a hairbrush.

As the attacks on allied shipping intensified, supplies of trawler fish dried up. Locally caught river fish, including salmon, started appearing on Benjamin's fish stall at the Butter Market. Rationing, meanwhile, meant everyone shared shortages in equal measure. Aileen Hepworth again:

Fishy Benjamin's: the fish stall at Hereford Butter Market during better days. Enemy submarine action saw river-caught fish replace supplies of sea fish. (*Herefordshire Lore/ In Our Age*)

Everybody had the same ration. Everyone was in the same boat. People used to help each other out. My grandad lived alone and my mother used to bake his bread and do his washing for him. We were sent twice a week to take him a loaf of bread and collect his washing.

The humble hen came to the rescue of many hungry households and canteens. By 1944 Hereford Training College had expanded to take in 140 student teachers, and trainee Elizabeth Newall remembered two Land Army girls being recruited to help on the now flourishing New Land kitchen gardens and orchard opposite the College. In 1943 the College had started horticultural courses under lecturer Miss Shrubsole, and a sty of pigs and a flock of hens were added to the College livestock. 'Anyone can give a lecture, but only a hen can lay a breakfast egg,' remarked one grateful foreign lecturer after a visit – and breakfast – at the College.

Eggs were a principal, and practical, part of a bomber crews' final meal before take-off, recalled Brian Davies:

> There was always a bacon and egg pre-bombing meal. You were warned that you were on a trip and then the timescale would come in 'meal at whatever', perhaps three o'clock in the afternoon, briefing, and then an hour out on the aircraft before you had a taxi time.

Good chooks: a Longtown housewife with her productive hens.
(*Richard Jenkins/ Winnie Reece*)

The reason for the bacon and egg meal was physiological. We were flying war machines [designed] to carry bombs and we had none of this pressurisation you get in modern aircraft. We used to operate at 20,000 feet and apart from the fact that it was mandatory to breathe oxygen at over 10,000 feet – and mandatory at night from the word go – the pressure outside [the aircraft] was very often less than the internal pressure. All sorts of funny 'noises' and smells used to drift through the aircraft. Hence the bacon and eggs, because anything else, beans or greens for example ...'

Eggs were once again on the menu for those air crews fortunate enough to return from these sorties. 'When we came back, we'd have bacon and eggs for breakfast with one exception: when you did your last trip you came back to bacon and eggs and a crate of light ale.'

Brian Davies was less impressed with the standard of food at RAF Shobdon. Before he left to train as a bomber pilot, Brian served as a glider pilot instructor at the station. The pilots were fed by the Navy, Army and Air Force Institutes, the NAAFI:

We seemed to exist for a long time on cheese and potato pie. So much so, that it took me around 60 years before I'd have cheese and potato pie again.

Bearing in mind that we were all young and swigging gallons of wartime beer (which was only half strength), we were probably more hung over at breakfast than at any other time of day. In the sergeants' mess there would be a plate of porridge, bread, a pat of margarine and a spoonful of marmalade. We used to throw the lot in the porridge bowl, mix it all up and sort of moisten it by pouring some tea on it. The tea, of course, was horrible because they had [put] bromide in there to reduce the sex drive.

The quality of the food improved considerably during the sergeants' mess dances, held every three months, leading Brian to suspect that the catering staff were, as he put it, 'on to a scam'.

Phyllis Edwards (formerly Phyllis Markey) from Lower Oldcroft near Lydney, defended the reputation of the NAAFI. She worked as a NAAFI cook, and 60 years after war had ended she could still consult her coverless and battered recipe book for a meat and potato pie, or a savoury omelette carefully costed out as '32 portions at 2d a portion'. Phyllis was employed as a maid in service at Cheltenham before the war. Now aged 17½ , she became a general assistant at the NAAFI kitchens at the training station, RAF Innsworth. 'I don't know if we were ever rationed, but 17-72-R was the number of our NAAFI building and I stayed working there until I was 23.' Under the watchful eye of manageress Margarita Smith, and nicknamed Sally to distinguish her from another Phyllis, she worked in the kitchen, surrounded by stoves, boilers, pots and pans. A shuttered counter opened out on to the canteen where a constant crush of trainee Air Force men and women gathered to collect their meals, or meet up for the regular concerts and dances. 'I was always very happy there,' recalled Phyllis who liked to patronise a café next door known as Smoky Joe's, or grab her cycle and head off. 'We used to bike for miles and miles on our days off, or we would go into Churchdown to the Vicars Ball: the vicar used to put on a dance of a Saturday night.'

Phyllis enjoyed cooking. Untrained and unqualified – 'I'd got no papers to prove I could cook' – she became renowned for her cake-making. 'We used to get margarine in big cardboard containers and had special marge for puff pastry. I'd work all through the afternoon to make enough cakes on great big trays for night-time.'

At home, as abroad, there was a thriving black market. Don Glead's father farmed at Canon Bridge and helped with the construction of the airfield at Madley, soon to become No. 4 Radio School. Workers at the site were billeted on local families, and some repaid the kindnesses shown them by their hosts with 'gifts' from the NAAFI. Coffee was in short supply, but before long catering-sized bottles of Camp Coffee appeared on the Glead's kitchen table:

> If we helped them they'd return the favour, come back with a bottle of coffee: that kept Mother going a long time.
>
> We'd generally have a young couple and two children, or perhaps a workman billeted on us. If you had just one man, he'd be in for meals when he came back from work; however if it was a family they'd have their own rations.

Hard cash could purchase most items: 'There were certain things on the black market that you could get hold of, especially round the towns. The spivs always had something to sell. Some of them, you got to watch them because they'd sell you something and it would be no use to you whatever.'

Phyllis Yapp's family, who ran the Builders Arms at Bearwood, helped to feed the men building RAF Shobdon:

> Mother used to have up to eight workers staying overnight for bed and breakfast. They loved coming there. Mother would cook fresh eggs, home cured bacon and fried bread. We'd have a side of pork hanging up and you used to get it down and slice if off: oh, the smell of that cooking in the morning!

One popular pastime was managing the illegal pig club. Contributors pooled their money to pay for the purchase and raising of a pig, which was duly slaughtered and the meat distributed quietly amongst the donors. On at least one occasion, however, the pig club members discovered they had been duped: there was no pig.

War threw up some gastronomic surprises. At the outbreak of war, Bill Dean was, as a private gardener, in a reserved occupation (that is, exempt from military service). 'We had to dig up the owner's lawns for potatoes. We planted Aran Pilot as early; Majestic was an old favourite, while King Edward was a soft potato that the slugs liked, although it was a good one for mashing.' However, by 1941 circumstances had changed. Bill had enlisted and was manning an anti-aircraft gun aboard a light cruiser, HMS *Glasgow*, acting as a convoy escort in the Mediterranean. Rations on board were, he judged, 'a bit rough'. They improved with the addition of exotics such as oranges and chocolate when he transferred to the troopship RMS *Mauretania* at Durban. At one point, however, they survived on tinned rations, which were something of a mystery. 'The tins came from a ship sunk at Tobruk. They'd recovered the tins, but none had any labels so you never knew what you were getting.' When, eventually, he reached Sicily he was astonished to see the generous rations given out to a black American brigade, the 92nd. Bill looked on in wonder: 'They even had fridges.'

Peter Holman, the son of a Kington police officer, recalled the generosity of the Americans when they arrived to set up camp near the town. 'The soldiers threw sweets and gum to people lining the streets to welcome them. Their military police worked closely with our police and my father invited one American to tea. They weren't rationed like us, but they only had powdered eggs at Hergest so my mother made him fresh fried eggs. We were horrified to see him put a load of homemade jam on them.' When the war came to an end the Americans invited every child in the town to a Camp party: 'We scoffed food and ice creams we had not seen for years.'

Land work: As the war dragged on, the Women's Land Army arrived to help with the harvests, as here at Court Farm, Rushall. (*Doreen Pocknell*)

4 The Women's Land Army

Formed in the closing years of the First World War, the Women's Land Army was revived in June 1939. Initially a voluntary organisation tasked with sending women to replace farm labourers who had left for the forces, the WLA eventually started conscripting women. 'We knew we had to do something,' recalled Marie Hill, who left her clerical job with building firm Bolts and joined the women working on the munitions: 'It was either that or join the Land Army.' The WLA was headed up by Lady Denman (she was also president of the National Federation of Women's Institutes) and would carry through after the war, disbanding in October 1949.

Female conscription: Land workers cleaning up for the dairy on a Herefordshire farm. (*Bobbie Blackwell*)

Recruitment posters for the WLA hinted at a balmy, bucolic and fun time for the land girls: 'For a healthy, happy job, Join the WLA' and 'A healthy open-air life …' . At least one poster featured Topsy Price from Ross-on-Wye. Topsy had joined the WLA in 1939 and spent a month in training at Usk College. Her first posting was to a farm near Chepstow where she learned to drive the boss's Fordson tractor, mastered the complexities of the mechanical hay cutter and worked from dawn until dusk. 'It was very, very hard work and the hours were long.' However,

Poster girl: Topsy Price from Ross featured on a wartime recruitment poster for the Women's Land Army. Life as a land girl, however, was demanding and arduous: 'It was very, very hard work.' (*Topsy Price*)

Topsy's ready smile and dark curls caught the attention of a man from the Ministry of Information tasked with finding promotional material for the WLA. A photographer was sent to the farm and Topsy found herself portrayed, hands on the wheel of the Fordson, on a WLA recruitment poster. As a consequence she was not surprised when another photographer asked her to pose for publicity pictures in 1940. She later received a set of glossy prints … and a visit from the military police. The cameraman, she was told, was an enemy agent who had been using Topsy as a front in order to photograph a munitions factory in the background.

Life in the WLA was never to be as romantic as people made out. Bobbie Blackwell spoke to several

former WLA women: 'Young women often found themselves in remote and isolated places, working very hard and for little reward.'

Around two-thirds of the recruits came from country homes. They were country women like Joy Atkins from Aylesbury, whose farm work days almost ended abruptly in the spring of 1940: 'I was raking hay with a horse rake on Herefordshire auctioneer Mr Baldwin's farm at Upper Sapey when the horse spooked. He began walking back before I could pull up the rake and I fell down between [the horse and the rake].' She only managed to scramble free when the man pitching the hay grabbed the wayward horse. In another moment the heavy rake would have run her over. 'I was ever grateful to him: he enabled me to enjoy seven years with the Women's Land Army.'

The rest of the WLA arrived on their farms as raw city recruits. They included Birmingham-born Kitty Latham whose initial efforts to become

'For a healthy happy job, join the Women's Land Army': Eve Lichfield (*above, centre*) at Redhill Hostel with her Land Army chums, Doris Hayes (*left*) and Jean McGaw (*right*). (*Bobbie Blackwell*)

Eve, Doris and Jean popped up again in this photo of Audrey Lowe and friends (*below*). Audrey Wilding, as she became, (*third row back, second right*) joined the WLA from Derbyshire. (*Ami Hartland*)

a Land Army woman were frustrated at every turn. 'I wanted to join, but my mother was against the idea.' Several months went by and an exasperated Kitty found herself working in the smart restaurant of Birmingham's Barrows Stores, founded by the Cadbury family and catering to stylish city clientele. At the end of her shift one day she approached the manager: 'I asked if I could leave and join the WLA. "Oh my dear," she said, "You are in essential work." Even the cook told me: "You're needed here." I thought if I hear that again I'll go mad.'

Essential Work: Kitty Latham, one of the women on parade with the WLA, wanted to quit her job, waitressing at Birmingham's Barrow Stores restaurant, but her manager told her: 'We need you here.' Eventually Kitty wrote a letter to the WLA and was immediately recruited and posted to Lower Lyde farm. (*Kitty Latham*)

By the time she reached 20 years of age, and sensing war slipping by, Kitty took the initiative and wrote directly to the WLA headquarters at Denman College asking for a posting. 'They sent me all this literature and [a letter]: "If you collect your uniform at such and such a date". That was it. I was a Land girl.' Kitty was interviewed by a Mr Park at Moorlands Farm at Kineton, Warwickshire – 'a nice old gentleman, an editor for one of the London papers' – and then dispatched to a busy farm where, after shadowing the men carrying out their different duties, she was put to work in the dairy:

> My prime job was to milk and do odd-jobs round the fields so the men could be released for heavier work. It was hands to the plough all the time. "Grow more of this, more of that, more of the other," but I loved it, every minute of it.

Doris Went was also employed in the dairy. She worked in Hereford itself, milking the cows at the city dairy, Bartonsham in St James. 'We started at six in the morning, hand-milking, on the stool, head in the flank and away to go! Then we delivered the milk with a can and a cart pulled by a horse called Tommy.'

Doris, like many other young women, fibbed about her age in order to join up: 'I wanted to get in the Land Army, but you had to be 18 so I bumped my age up a bit. I was sent to work at Hay Lane Farm, Leominster, and I met my future husband there.' Later she was sent to work at Bartonsham.

Like Doris, many women founded their families during their days with the WLA. Kitty Latham became engaged to a young man who was employed on secret war work at Barronia Metals in Hereford (*see 'Barronia', page 81*). They moved to Hereford, married, and Kitty returned to land work at Lower Lyde. 'I was hoeing mangles, taking them into the barns and putting them through the chaffing machine.' Kitty recalled how the farmer recruited extra labour, sending a tractor and a dray to the College Estate in Hereford every day to collect women and their younger children to work. When it was time to return home the children were discreetly dispatched to the orchard and potato store by their mums.

> These kids would come back to where the tractor was waiting, but they'd a job to climb into the dray because of the weight they were carrying in the bottoms of their coats with all the apples and potatoes. It was the funniest thing I have ever seen. They were like Ken Dodd's Diddy Men.

Land Army girl Kathleen married her sweetheart Joe Wade in 1945. Joe would captain Arsenal football club in the 1950s and later became a popular player-manager at Hereford United. He first played for Hereford in 1945–46 which was where he met WLA girl Kathleen. Agricultural engineer Basil Morgan also met his future wife, May, when the 18-year-old came down from her native Yorkshire to work with the WLA at Pigeon House Farm in Kilpeck.

Upper Sapey's John Thacker also made a match with a land girl, Shirley. He recalled working alongside Shirley in 1943 on the Old Hopyard, a field at Boswick Farm in Wolferlow: 'In those days the seeds were singled out in the rows with a hoe by hand.' Shirley, however, was helping to 'scuffle' the sugar beet, fighting to manage the horse-drawn one-row hoe, which was working between the rows, pulled by the old cart-horse called, ironically, Lively. 'The Boss was there, but he wasn't in a very good mood,' recalled John:

> At the end of the rows the headland wasn't wide enough and Shirley kept catching off the last beet in the row. "You got to get the horse's head right up in the hedge before you turn the scuffle round", he told her. Eventually Shirley got the hang of it and when she returned with Lively the boss was smiling.
>
> He offered her his tobacco tin and when she opened it she found a gold sovereign: she'd scuffled it up on the headland. I often wondered about the poor hop picker who, in years gone by, must have dropped and lost his sovereign in the Old Hopyard.

Many land girls were accommodated at hostels such as Redhill, a hostel on the outskirts of Hereford city, which housed thousands of war workers (*see 'Redhill Hostel', page 65*). The WLA's Rose Ellerton, having collected her uniform from the issuing officer Maud Wills at her Offa Street office, found herself billeted at Redhill with her friend Joan Thomas who joined the Timber Corps (*see 'The Lumber Jills', page 33*). Joan recalled a rare day off when Rose was preparing to go out on the town with her boyfriend Derek. A third friend, coming up to the hostel from the canteen, noticed Derek's arrival – he was chatting to friends by the bicycle stands – and she called on Rose to tell her so.

Joan took up the story:

> Thinking she might be some time, Rose slipped out to ask Derek to wait, but as she was in the middle of a full wash down she had no clothes on. She grabbed her Land Army coat and slipped into it for a respectable cover up. When she neared the bicycle stands she could see several airmen chatting together. She pulled her coat further round her as she passed them by, forgetting the vent at the back of the coat. The airmen burst into laughter as she walked past. "Were they laughing at me being in my curlers?" she asked Derek. "No", said Derek, "They wouldn't be looking at your head!"

While Rose stayed at Redhill Hostel, others were billeted on farms, sometimes in difficult circumstances. Maureen Gilbert's family ran the farm at Bullinghope. 'My father, Roy Lloyd, worked at Green Crize Nurseries growing tomatoes with the help of two land girls, Joyce and Winnie.' The women lived in at the farmhouse along with two other WLA women billeted there: all four shared a single bed, two at the top and two at the bottom.

Nancy Price from Stoke was initially put up in a hostel after enlisting with the WLA:

> When I joined I was met at Ross, along with some other city girls, and driven to a hostel in the countryside. No messing about: next morning we were handed bib and brace overalls, black high-top boots, and a hoe for our first job. So, lots of blisters and sore backs, but we toughed it out. A few days later we were dropped off at different farms then back to the hostel for the night. With farmers needing full-time help, you could choose to live in at the farmhouse.

Nancy chose to stay with Mr and Mrs Josephs at Whitfield Court in Glewstone, where she worked alongside Rolf, a German prisoner of war (he stayed in Ross, being dropped off for work each day). Although miles away from home, Nancy enjoyed her new life on the land:

Making a match: farm work around Ross involved 'lots of blisters and sore backs,' recalled Nancy Price, above with Land Army friends at Whitfield Court, Glewstone. But life in the WLA had its compensations: Nancy's came in the form of husband-to-be Tom and his BSA motorbike. (Nancy Price)

> I fell in love, not only with the beautiful countryside, but with Tom Price from the adjoining farm, Little Whitfield. Tom drove a BSA motorbike – wow!! – and our courtship started with local dances, trips to Symonds Yat and to Lower Common Farm at Mitchel Troy to meet Mum and Dad Price.

Return to work: Mavis Matthews was evacuated to Herefordshire from her home in Liverpool (*see 'Evacuees', page 71*). As soon as she was old enough she joined the WLA and, having learned to drive, took command of a three-ton lorry to ferry WLA girls around the county farms. (*Mavis Matthews*)

They married, and seven years later emigrated to Canada.

For Liverpool-born Mavis Owen (now Matthews), evacuated to Herefordshire in 1941, the WLA represented her best opportunity to return to the county she loved. She joined in June 1947. 'I learned to drive at Oxford then came to Hereford and stayed at Redhill Hostel driving the girls to work. I said to the sergeant in charge one day: "Why don't I take a lorry? I could carry more girls."' She was put behind the wheel of a three-ton delivery truck, which she fetched and returned to the depot on Ross Road each day.

One of the regular passengers was Daphne Tillam who, with husband Gerry, went on to run the Royal George in Widemarsh Street after the war. She served with the WLA in 1947, living at Redhill Hostel and meeting her husband-to-be at the YMCA in St Owen Street. 'His parents had a butcher's shop opposite the Lamb Hotel and he and I later started Hereford's first mini-cab business.'

Women like Daphne would have to wait a long time for any official recognition of their wartime work: it was not until 2007, 60 years after they had been disbanded, that the WLA were issued with badges that acknowledged their services. Even then some failed to receive a badge. Nottingham-born Jeanne Glover came to live in Hereford towards the end of her life. She had served with the WLA on farms in Shropshire during the last war. Jeanne recalled meeting her husband-to-be, American GI Tony Picciana, one evening after work at the Red Lion in Costock, Shropshire. 'Mum was playing the piano for the soldiers when Tony approached her and asked: "Who's the blonde in the corner?"

"Keep away! That's my daughter," declared Mum.'

It was to no avail and Tony Picciana and Jeanne were married shortly before he left for the D-Day landings. A paratrooper with the 507th, Tony would fight on Omaha Beach and help liberate one of the Nazi concentration camps. When peace came he returned to New York, Jeanne following later aboard the SS *Washington*. After Tony's

GI bride: Land Army girl Jeanne Glover met and married U.S. paratrooper Tony Picciana and moved to the States to live with him. When Tony died she returned to England. Herefordshire Lore's Peter Mayne (*above left*) helped her claim her Women's Land Army badge. (*Herefordshire Lore/ In Our Age*)

death, Jeanne came back to England, moving to Charles Court in Putson. Herefordshire Lore's Peter and Jean Mayne helped her apply for that missing medal. 'Wonderful!' was Jeanne's comment when it was finally presented.

Aside from the WLA, many women did unpaid work 'on the clods', as city mum Katy Deem recalled. She was a 'ganger', a foreman in charge of a party of Emergency Land Corps women who would head out to work on different farms after finishing their day job. Audrey Morgan, for example, worked at the War Agricultural offices in St John Street; while her friends, sisters Win and Ruby Philpotts were employed at Greenlands department store. 'Early evenings we would be taken to a farm to do a few hours work. We enjoyed ourselves,' Audrey remembered.

Katy recalled boarding the 'War-Ag' lorry, their gas masks piled together in a pillow slip: 'We'd say to the driver: "Which clods are we going on today?" It was all voluntary.' Katy and her mates also helped the hospitals as well as the farmers. 'When we were hop picking, they used to get the biggest crib [the crib held the picked hops] and everybody put an hour's picking in. That was done for the hospitals.'

After her working day in the glass department at Greenlands, Ruby would find herself hop tying or weeding. 'We weren't told where we were going because of the war and we didn't get paid. But it was a lovely atmosphere, everyone working towards something.' Later in the war Ruby left to become a porter guard on the railways, delivering parcels and freight across the country with the Great Western Railway and London Midlands Service.

5   The Lumber Jills

A THIRD OF BRITAIN'S WOODLANDS WOULD BE FELLED TO FEED THE WARTIME demand for timber. Neighbouring districts such as the Forest of Dean were seriously affected. In 1942 the Forestry Commission was tasked with setting up a Women's Timber Corps to provide extra labour for work in the woods and sawmills. The Women's Land Army had taken control of the WTC and its 'lumber Jills' when Shropshire-born Joan Thomas opted to join their ranks. Following in the footsteps of her twin sister Joyce, Joan joined the Timber Corps. She was dispatched to Hereford. 'We were very colourful with our vivid green pullovers and bright green berets,' she recalled,

> Both the Land Army and the Timber Corps had green and gold badges with a wheat sheaf in the centre, but the Timber Corps also had a dark brown Bakelite cap badge with a tree as the centrepiece. Crossed axes also distinguished us from the Land Army: the axes adorned the arms of our greatcoats, while similar axes in felt were worn on the arms of our green pullovers.

Practical as it was, the uniform had other advantages. 'The Americans were intrigued: "Gee! You girls are something else!"' Young women like Joan experimented with different ways of showing off their new attire: 'Our ties did not sit well with Aertex shirts, but they smartened up our Poplin shirts: the Aertex shirts were easy-care, but the Poplin ones looked better if you showed the collar and cuffs an iron occasionally.'

The beret came in for special attention:

> Our berets distinguished us from the Land Army's rather duller fawn-coloured brimmed hats. We liked our berets because they tolerated a variety of hairstyles and could be worn at jaunty angles. We could pull them forward or push them back so as not to flatten the more bouffant look.

Joan conceded that their best efforts did not always work. 'We could tilt the berets sideways or balance them aloft cheekily. But then you might be asked: "Have you got a stiff neck?" which was one way of saying: "Have you any idea how ridiculous you look?"'

The uniforms were collected from offices in Offa Street and included boots, leggings, riding breeches, six pairs of woollen knee socks and dungarees. They did not remain standard issue for long:

> Dungarees were worn to work in, and they became the forerunners of hot pants when we chopped the legs off as short as we dared for a touch of glamour in the summer. I'd never taken a lot of notice of legs before, thinking they were all much of a muchness, but my goodness, ours weren't. But it was easier to dry our legs after a downpour than it was to dry our clothes.
>
> Our greatcoats were fawn colour, three-quarter length, heavy and of a superior quality. There was a vent at the back for freedom of movement. The epaulets were useful for tucking our berets into, or preventing our shoulder bags from slipping. With perseverance and thick socks our sturdy brown shoes became wearable, though my feet never forgave me. They donated two enormous bunions and a couple of painful corns.

Joan's light-hearted look at their uniforms belied some hard work in the forests.

Twenty-two-year-old Marion Jones (née Moscrop) had left the comforts of her family home in Manchester to join the Timber Corps. Checking she had her identity card, ration book, clothing coupons, gas mask and spare uniform, she boarded the 10:42 Manchester train for Machynlleth. It was the first time she had left home.

A six-hour train journey brought Marion to the little station of Esgairgeiliog in the Afon Dulas valley near Machynlleth. As she recalled later in her self-published memoir, *Proud to be a Timber Girl*, she could neither pronounce her destination nor understand what the station staff were saying to one another: 'I was amazed to hear Welsh spoken everywhere.'

Initially, she and the other trainee forestry girls managed without Welsh, but when her companions were moved to other parts of the country Marion began to pick up enough of the language to get by. She was billeted with a Mrs Lloyd of Dulas Cottage, a residence with one downstairs room, two bedrooms and 'quite primitive toilet facilities in the cellar'. In return for 12 shillings a week, Mrs Lloyd put her up and cooked her meals. Marion bought the food.

In contrast to the open, bracken-covered hills of neighbouring Mid-Wales, the Dulas Valley was a dark-green, recently forested landscape.

Foreign fields: 22-year-old Marion Jones from Manchester joined the Timber Corps and was posted to the remote Dulas Valley. 'I was amazed to hear Welsh spoken everywhere.' (*Marion Jones*)

The Forestry Commission had been formed in 1919 to repair the devastation caused by the last world war on woodland stocks. In the intervening years the Commission had targeted these Welsh valleys, taking over the traditional tenanted hill farms of the Dovey and Corris district and planting them with fast-growing conifer plantations. 'Men who were tenant farmers became Forestry Commission smallholders. They kept their houses, a few fertile fields around them, but the rest of the land was planted,' recalled Marion. It was not necessarily a happy transition for these smallholders turned forestry workers. Marion quoted a poem, *The Alien*, by preacher and poet Morris J. Morris, the son of one former hill farmer:

> The old ways were erased
> By the natives of far away Scandinavia
> The region is under a green blanket
> No more we'll see the shepherd
> In Bwlch y Gwynt pass.

Shortly after arriving in the valley Marion watched the poet's father's funeral pass by, 'his coffin being carried, followed by the men of the valley walking behind over the mountain to Pantperthog chapel for the burial.' There was no road between farmhouse and village. For the next four years, from January 1942 to November 1946, Marion would live and work in this tight-knit, remote rural community. She would leave eventually and move to Hereford, having met and married her husband here.

For now, with the war overshadowing the forested valleys, Marion learned the forestry crafts. Wearing trousers and overalls for the first time in her life she and 12 other girls would set off in their heavy boots with their supervisor Charles Williams, or 'Charlie Ty Pwt' (named after his house, *ty*, where he was born), for a three-quarter-mile walk up Mynydd Fron-felen. Under sunny, sullen or wet skies ('we had such a lot of very wet weather') they worked to separate cordwood from the brushwood with hand axes. Some days were spent sawing and loading pit props: 'The work was hard and it sometimes poured with rain all day.' She took fright when she turned over a pit prop and encountered her first snake.

Like the other girls in the Timber Corps, Marion socialised and attended chapel (she went to the English chapel, *Y Capel Seisnig*, in Machynlleth), yet relations between the local people and these green city girls from England were often ambivalent. They worsened when the valley was struck by a forest fire. 'On a Saturday morning in early summer someone walking in the cwm saw smoke coming from the site where we had been burning [the previous day]. By the time he got down to the village to report the flames, the fire had taken hold.' For two days the fire burned out of control despite the efforts of the valley people who turned out to fight the blaze with fire-beaters. Eventually, when the fire reached the edge of the village, fire engines were able to pump water from the nearby river Dulas, douse the flames and bring the fire under control.

The timber girls were held responsible for the accident in spite of having been working under supervision and obediently doing as they were told. 'The timber girls were blamed and felt it very much. Although we were following all the rules we were truly sorry. This was an experience that I can never forget.'

Back in Hereford, lumber Jill Joan Thomas was busy breaking into the man's world of timber work. She arrived in Hereford, bound for Redhill Hostel (see 'Redhill Hostel', page 65) on 15 August 1942. A friend, Phyllis Green, who had joined with her was feeling homesick: 'She told me: "They cried when I left home this morning" and looked about to do the same. But then a lorry manned by girls in dungarees and Aertex shirts met us. Because we were new and were wearing skirts, we were allowed to sit in the lorry cab.' The truck and their new acquaintances, Betty and Iris ('Betty turned out to be a New Zealander, married to an army officer at Bradbury Lines') pulled up outside a milk bar in Commercial Street for a round of milk shakes before they headed off to the Hostel. The milk bar was run by farmer's daughter Jeanne Perkins from Ufton Court (see 'Subterfuge and Deception', page 133).

From then on:

> we worked from dawn to dusk in winter, and in the summer from dawn to early evening. One of our girls recalled how she once helped to chop a tree down in her garden at home and was drained for the rest of the day: she never thought then that she would be felling massive trees as a job.

As Joan recalled: 'The Timber Corps "didn't do drained"' so she just had to get on with it.

Eileen Lloyd, then a girl growing up at Wormelow, recalled how the New Zealand Forestry Corps, working in Mynde Wood, was based at the old Bryngwyn manor. 'Their cookhouse was by our Granny Thomas' fence and the children would be treated to iced buns and sweets. Later the mansion was used first by Italian and then German prisoners of war.'

The woodland work had its amusing moments. Lilian Kearne (then Lilian Speller) was working as a Timber Corps girl alongside a Gypsy family from Blakemere:

> They were a fine and proud family, hard-working, spotlessly clean – the inside of their caravan an absolute picture of tidiness.
>
> We were working in the wood one day when I thought I'd sit on one of their horses. What a width to straddle! One of the men nearby hit the animal across the rear end and the horse bolted with me hanging on for dear life. It eventually stopped and Ann [one of the Gypsy women] caught us up and helped me down. We were very shocked, she and I!

The Timber Corps was disbanded in 1946, each worker receiving a letter of thanks for their service from the Queen.

6   The Home Guard

E ARLY IN 1940 THE BRITISH EXPEDITIONARY FORCE WAS IN RETREAT AT DUNKIRK. France was expected to fall at any moment. Politicians and the press clamoured for a local defence force to protect Britain from invasion. There were calls for local rifle clubs to form combatant units and, specifically, for golfers to be trained in marksmanship, presumably so that they could shoot down enemy parachutists falling on the local links. On 14 May 1940 the Secretary of State for War, Anthony Eden, stepped in and announced the formation of the Local Defence Volunteers, later called the Home Guard. They were to act as a kind of armed police force, their role to slow up the enemy during the expected German attack, and to carry out guerrilla warfare in the event of an invasion.

Hcrefordshire men formed orderly queues to sign up. Aged between 17 and 65, men either too old or too young for the conventional forces, and those in reserved occupations, were soon in training across the country. They included First World War veterans such as Albert Mangham, the proprietor, with his wife Annie, of Ye Olde

His second war: a veteran of the First World War, Ledbury's Albert Mangham (seen here with his wife Annie and grandson Peter Holman) was quick to join the Local Defence Volunteers. (*Peter Holman*)

Flower Shop in Church Street, Ledbury. 'He had already served as a corporal in the Royal Garrison Artillery in France in the First World War,' recalled his grandson Peter Holman. Then, as now, this 'Dad's Army' was the butt of bad jokes: asked how he would recognize Hitler when the invasion came, the English comedian Robb Wilton quipped 'I've got a tongue in my head, haven't I?'

Yet the prospect that they might shortly be involved in hand-to-hand fighting with German soldiers was never far from their minds. Henry Moss' stepfather George Bywater was the wagoner at Aconbury Court. He was also a member of the local Home Guard, training every Sunday 'and often coming back the worse for drink afterwards'.

In training: Home Guard units, like this one on camp at the Callow, Hereford, were caricatured as charmingly incompetent by BBC television's *Dad's Army*. In reality, Home Guardsmen were steeling themselves to mount a final defence against the German invasion which was expected at any time. The men were prepared to fight to the bitter end. (*Bruce Leonard*)

Active service: Jim Lewis with daughter Anne in the gardens at Brockhampton Court where Jim worked as head gardener. He also served as Sergeant Lewis with Brockhampton Home Guard. (*Anne Milne*)

Henry clearly remembered the ominous sound of German bombers flying over Aconbury:

Leaving church to walk home, we could see the searchlights at the top of the Callow picking them up as flares or anti-aircraft fire lit up the night sky. Later, Father took us outside as the night sky was lit up by the first night of the Blitz on Liverpool. Two nights later Swansea was bombed and that also lit up our night sky. Mother told me to say a prayer for those in the cities.

The German bombers were seen as a prelude to the arrival of ground troops – a sobering thought.

Jim Lewis, head gardener at Brockhampton Court, provided food and flowers for owner Mrs Clay and raised vital supplies of onion seed for the leading horticultural company of the time, Carter's Tested Seeds of Raynes Park

Pony power: Brockhampton's 14th Platoon of the 5th Battalion, Hereford Home Guard. The photographer, Vivians, listed the men as: (*back row, left to right*) Pte Allsopp (*mounted*), Ptes White, Powell, Cotterell, Sollars, W.G. Yarnold, Lamont, H.C. Lilley and Meredith; (*third row*) Ptes Parsons, E. Maddox, Hope, Lerigo, Davies, Hall, R. Clarke, A.H. Howells, E. Clarke, A. Lilley; (*second row*) Pte Ford, Captain Pearson, Sgt Philips, Sgt Colburn, Lt H.B. Eccles, Sgt Jim Lewis, Sgt Hale, Captain Hudson, Ptes J.C. Howells, Avery; (*front*) Ptes Scaffold, Mapp, D. Maddox, R.G. Yarnold, Joslyn, Winter, White, Baldwin, Parry, Green. (*Anne Milne*)

near London. Jim also served as Sergeant with the Brockhampton Home Guard, the 14th Platoon of the 5th Battalion of the Hereford Home Guard. His daughter Anne, then a school girl in Ross, recalled watching her father train with his comrades. She was intrigued by the army-issue black-and-white rifle targets; how they flipped over when hit.

Anne's school, Highfield, occupied the Red House in Palmerston Road, having been evacuated from Gorleston-on-Sea in Norfolk by headmistress Miss Cleo Blank and her dog Chum over fears of an invasion (several schools were moved to Herefordshire during the war, including Felsted School in Essex, which occupied Hillcourt and Pencraig Courts, and St Philips from Birmingham).

The war ministry had ordered that, in the event of an invasion, church bells, silenced at the outbreak of hostilities, would be sounded. 1940 was marked by constant false alarms, and on one occasion the bell of Brockhampton church rang out following rumours of an impending attack by German parachutists. The ringer, tolling the bell with his back to the church door, nearly died of fright when the Home Guardsman, sent to stand him down, tapped him on the shoulder.

"A" COMPANY, 3rd HEREFORDSHIRE (HEREFORD CITY) BATTALION HOME GUARD

Standing guard: Home Guard units, such as Tupsley's, had a range of duties, from protecting strategic sites to shooting down V-1 'doodlebugs'. Guardsman Derek Adams did both, firing on V-1s crossing the south coast, and mounting guard at a fatal crash site in Tupsley. These guardsmen, with Linda Griffin's father Bill Griffin (*third from right, second row at the back*), were photographed in 1941/42. (*Linda Griffin*)

The duties of the Home Guardsmen, varied as they were, were serious enough. Early in 1940, Vera Parry from Newtown heard of a young RAF trainee getting into difficulties during his first solo flight over the village:

> He [had] landed safely in a field opposite our house – no mean feat as there was a commemorative oak surrounded by an iron frame bang in the middle of the field. He went across to the New Inn, later the Barneby Inn, and reported to base. He was told not take off, but to return to base.

The local Home Guard were called out to watch the aircraft, day and night, and on Monday morning they assisted the experienced pilot who had arrived to bring home the plane, a twin-engine Airspeed Oxford, with his take off procedures. The Guard and villagers then watched the pilot taxi towards the south-west:

> We knew that the field dropped steeply away towards the stream, but of course we couldn't interfere with the operation. Then, to our horror we saw the plane crash into an oak tree near Lower Brockington. The adults rushed down (we teenagers were discouraged). Somewhile later we saw the body of the pilot being carried up to New Inn on a field gate. Someone walked beside it carrying a single long boot.

Another Home Guardsman who witnessed an airplane crash was Derek Adams. He was cycling to a Guard meeting on Hampton Dene Road in Tupsley one day when he saw a training plane from RAF Madley crash at the Knoll, a large house in Church Road. When he went to investigate he was ordered by Major Bailey, the Knoll's owner, to guard the plane until the RAF could take it away. He stood on guard for four hours, acutely aware of the flying helmet of the unfortunate pilot who had been killed showing above ground where the plane had plunged into the earth. The crash killed both the pilot, Bill Binnie and trainee radio operator, Corporal Nutter (*see 'The War Above', page 97*).

In anticipation of the guerrilla fighting and the house-to-house battles that would ensue when the Germans arrived, the Home Guard was trained in street fighting. Derek, unable to serve in the regular forces because of his deafness, had joined the C Company, 3rd Herefordshire (Hereford City) Battalion Home Guard, based at the Rose and Crown in Ledbury Road. C Company used the quarry and brick works, now designated a 'live fire exercise area', at Tupsley for street warfare training.

The training did not always go to plan. John Slatford also served with the Tupsley Home Guard, which paraded every Sunday at the Rose and Crown on the Ledbury Road. He recalled one training event that went spectacularly wrong, twice. 'Sergeant Harry Powell was giving instructions on using an anti-tank weapon, a Blacker Bombard mortar, aiming it at his own house, 11 Church Road, 400 yards away,' John recalled. 'Whether he intended to or not, he fired the missile [it could not have contained explosive] and hit

Pot shot: There were red faces among the Tupsley Guardsmen when an anti-tank training exercise at the Rose and Crown went spectacularly wrong. Trialling a Blacker Bombard mortar, Sergeant Harry Powell accidentally hit his own house with the first round and a neighbour's with the second. The 3rd Herefordshire A Company (Hereford City) are pictured (*above*), possibly outside Bishops School, with Bill Young (*centre, back row*), and in training at Tupsley (*below*). (*Ann Johnstone and Michael Young*)

the target! The damage was not too serious and no-one was hurt, whereupon a second bomb was fired, hitting a neighbour's house and inflicting greater damage.'

It was not the only accident to befall the Guard. Harry Powell's daughter Margaret recalled her older brother, John, accidentally dropping an item of equipment on the kitchen floor. It exploded with a loud report, breaking crockery and rendering the whole family stone-deaf for 24 hours.

Home Guard units did their best to aid civilians caught up in enemy bombing raids. Munitioneer Marjorie Powell was just finishing her night shift at Rotherwas Munitions Factory in July 1942:

Local Defence Volunteers (LDV): formed in 1940 after the Allied retreat from Dunkirk, the LDV, as the Home Guard was initially known, was open to men aged between 17 and 65. The Guardsmen, like these men from Clehonger and Allensmore Home Guard pictured outside cider makers Ridler and Son at Clehonger, served without pay. Sid Dykes (*far left*) worked for Ridler and, as a farm labourer, was exempt from military service. He and his wife Lilian had moved back to Herefordshire after a spell on a Surrey farm. (*Annie Lilwall*)

I was working on the 25lb bombs and we were in the canteen on the north side when the Home Guard came in. "Get on the bloody floor: Jerry's here," they shouted. I didn't want to be stuck inside a bombed-out building so I ran outside. Just then one of the bombs exploded and it knocked me right back inside the canteen.' (*see 'On the Munitions', page 85*).

Suffering minor cuts, Marjorie escaped serious injury, but witnessed some terrible injuries in one woman pulled from the wreckage. The following year Marjorie had a second escape when the late-night film show at the Roxy in Ross led to her missing the morning work bus by minutes: 'I stayed home working in the St Owens Cross pub where we lived when we heard a loud rumble.' Later she learned that one of the 25lb bombs in the section where she normally worked had exploded.

As the war ground on, the Home Guard was sometimes used to relieve regular soldiers. When infantrymen guarding the south coast at Shorncliffe near Folkestone were given two weeks leave, an appeal went out for Home Guardsmen with a reputation for accurate shooting, to stand in for the infantrymen. Lance Corporal Derek Adams volunteered: he was a sharp shot having recently won £10 at an intercompany shooting exercise at Middle Park, Fownhope. When he arrived at Shorncliffe he discovered

Cusop Home Guard (*left*): although often short of uniforms and arms, several guardsmen had secret training in sabotage and hand-to-hand killing, and assisted the covert Auxiliary Units, set up in the summer of 1940. These Cusop guardsmen included (*back row*) Raymond Smith, Charlie Williams, Trevor Lloyd; (*front*) Herbie Williams, Charles Parry, Herbert Parry, Captain Hissey, Gordon Williams, Charlie Watkins and Harry Brook, headmaster of Clifford School. (*Eric Pugh*)

Castle Frome: the Home Guard No. 18 Platoon D Company, 2nd Battalion Herefordshire Home Guard. Janet Lloyd, whose grandmother Maggie Dutson ran the Green Dragon at Bishops Frome, recalled how the men often met in the pub's hop store. 'They mostly came to the Dragon for a drink afterwards.' (*Back row, left to right*) Turner, Turner, Stan Dutson (Wellington Farm), not known, Harry Airs, Bill Dutson (Birches Farm), Edward Pudge, Tom Bullock (The Town House, Castle Frome). (*Middle row*) Harry Hill, John Griffiths, Harold Simcox (Richley Farm), Bert Morris, Scotty Bowler (haulage contractor), Rowland Greenwood (farmer), Jeff Bray, Jack Hill. (*Front*) Parker (farmer), Reg Bray, Frank Symonds (garage owner), Pillinger (Chase Inn), Farr, Bigley, Jack Phillips. (*Louise Manning*)

that one of his duties was to try and bring down the flying bombs or 'doodlebugs', unmanned V-1 missiles that were being sent over to attack London.

He and his men were issued with a Browning automatic and 40 rounds of ammunition, which they rapidly used up as the rockets passed overhead. Billeted in the regular soldiers' barracks during their stay on the coast, Derek noted with apprehension the shrapnel holes left in the barracks' roof following their earlier efforts.

Stood down: Ada Durrant of Vivians, the Hereford High Town photographer, regularly photographed military personnel. She was on hand to capture the farewell parade of the Much Marcle Home Guard when they were stood down on 3 December 1944. The 5th Hereford Battalion Home Guard: (*back row, left to right*) Lt Powell, 2/Lt Barber, Lts Clarke, Davies, Watson, Greenhill, Thompson, Capt. Waller, Lt Parry, 2/Lts Hawkins, Boughey, Lt Ree, Capt. Allwright, Lt Summers. (*Third row*) Lt Taylor, 2/Lt Mitchell, Capt. Farr, 2/Lts Dougherty and Hill, Lt Eccles, Major Turner, Lts Denness, Gardner, Birtwistle and Warren. (*Second row*) Lts Hicks, Weston, Randall, Madders, Bristow, Blakemore, Lucas, 2/Lt Tyler, Capt. Bickham, Major Goldie, Lt Phillips. (*Front*) Adjt Capt. Wright, Sir Sidney Clive, Majors Farrow and Morland, Lt-Col Toynbee (Commanding Officer), The Lord Ruthven, Major Spankie, Capt. Raymond, Quartermaster Capt. Silver. (*Gordon Armand*)

Postal power: the General Post Office (GPO) Home Guard in Hereford. (*Peter Mayne*)

Eventually, with the Germans fighting a losing battle on the eastern front against Russia, the threat of invasion began to subside. The Home Guard continued to operate after the allied D-Day landings in June 1944, before finally being stood down that December. Years later the *Dad's Army* image of the Home Guard, perpetuated by BBC television's popular comedy series of the same name, portrayed a lovable, but incompetent fighting force. However, Derek Adams remained convinced that if Britain had been invaded, the Home Guard would have formed an efficient and effective resistance determined to defend their families and homes to the bitter end.

7 Buses, Trains and Bikes

WOMEN HAD BROKEN INTO ANOTHER ALL-MALE BASTION BY THE MIDDLE OF THE war: they were 'manning' the buses. Bill Thomas of Foley Street, one of the first bus drivers in the city and a man who fastidiously polished his leather belt and boots before heading for the depot, now found himself teaching women to drive. Petrol-engine buses had to be hand-cranked to start: 'no mean feat on a cold winter's morning – some had a kick like a mule', recalled his son Jim. In deference to the women, diesel-engined buses equipped with electrical starter motors were chosen for the women drivers.

Among Bill's first learner-drivers were Winnie Tranter and Katy Nash. Katy was taken on in 1941 and she would recall later, to Richard Dimbleby on BBC radio's *Down Your Way* programme, how she went on to drive for the Midland Red for the next 22 years.

Forty-two-year old Dorothy Jones from Westfields, Hereford was, in the early days of the war, delivering bread from a cart pulled by a horse called Bess for the Roberts' family (the Roberts ran the Café Royal in St Peters Street). Dorothy left to join the Midland Red as a conductress, becoming their first lady 'clippie'. She was kept busy. While railways moved the war along, it was the buses that kept people moving at home. 'There were more people going on the buses because of petrol rationing,' remembered conductor Stan Fryer.

Clippie Edna Jarvis rode the buses, with her ticket punch and a bunch of tickets held together with an elastic band. She took on the country rides to Hay and other longer, out-of-county journeys. 'The farthest we went was Shrewsbury and Worcester, and the buses were full nine times out of ten. It was hard work, mind, but everyone seemed to be happier in those days, there was no arguments.'

The busy buses did occasionally lead to disagreements. When Bromyard's Norman Allen returned from the fighting in Burma

Back from Burma: There was no room on the Birmingham bus for Bromyard's Norman Allen, home from fighting in Burma, despite the pleas of his wife. (*Christine Millard*)

All aboard: A Midland Red bus in High Town, Hereford in 1948. (*Michael Young*)

(the war with Germany was already over) his wife met him at Snow Hill Station in Birmingham. According to their daughter Christine Millard, the couple headed off for the No. 70 bus stop:

> They were standing there, him with his kit bag, waiting for the bus. But when the bus arrived, the conductor wouldn't let them on as it was getting full. My mother said: "But he's just come back from Burma!" However the conductor would still not let them get on.

In acknowledgement of their wartime roles, the bus women's outfits were given a military look. 'The uniform was like an army uniform except that it was navy and you had a belt and cap like the ATS [Auxiliary Territorial Service],' recalled Edna.

Fares were straightforward: 'It was three halfpence to come up to Hunderton from the town [Hereford] although the fares were two-and-a-half pence to most places' – and the pay was higher than for women in domestic service: 'It seemed like good money to us in them days.'

When there were insufficient men or women to work the buses, the operators were recruited from school. Stan Fryer was allowed out of the classroom at Llangarron School to join Percy Tumney's local bus service as a conductor. Stan was just twelve.

The railways, too, were busier than ever now, transporting military personnel, arms and munitions as well as civilians and the normal freight. They also brought home the wounded. Frances Coleman recalled walking from Hereford railway station and seeing lines of soldiers along Station Road. 'This was after Dunkirk and they were waiting to be transported to various places for kitting out and rejoining their national armies. They were so quiet, tired and, I think, dispirited, I didn't even get a [wolf] whistle.' Later in the war Kit Gower – Taffy to her friends – had a similar experience in Leicester. The 17-year-old Lugwardine girl had joined the Auxiliary Territorial Service and was on escort duties when the first wounded soldiers began returning from the Normandy landings. 'There were terrible injuries, men with no legs, no arms. I remember putting cigarettes between their lips and lighting them for them.'

Royal train: King George VI (*centre, second from left*) seen here visiting Ledbury before the war, arrived in the county by train in October 1941. He stopped at Leominster and Barrs Court stations for official duties before being driven on to Monmouth by car. The motorcade, however, halted outside the New Inn at St Owens Cross. 'We heard the King was coming by to decorate some General', recalled Marjorie Powell whose father ran the Inn. 'I'd gone down into the kitchen and was looking through the window and there he was!'' The King rejoined the royal train at Monmouth after reviewing troops from the 18th Infantry Division shortly before they left for the Far East. The Division would be wiped out by the Japanese after the fall of Singapore. (*Peter Holman*)

Marjorie (*left*) with little Jack, Nancy, father Albert behind, Cecil, and mother Kate holding baby Bill. (*Marjorie Powell*)

Trusty steed: Eleanor Gilbert (later Eleanor English) from Bishopstone with her bike (*left*), made in a Worcester factory before the business was requisitioned to make ammunition. Everyone relied on their bikes, including these Canadian soldiers (*above*) at Garnons with Eleanor (*centre, with bike*), then 22 years old and a member of the Auxiliary Territorial Service. (*Susannah Garland*)

John 'Brecky' Davies had joined the Great Western Railway as a 14-year-old lad porter 'doing the odd jobs like cleaning all the signal lamps' in 1942. 'Because it was the war I was put in as engine cleaner doing the shedman's job, putting the coal on the engine, dropping the fires (at the end of the day) and preparing them for the following day.' Davies was also the 'knocker-up', waking the railwaymen 'in the blackout, no light anywhere'. Three years later he was sent to Bristol, an impressively busy terminus – 'there were over 1,000 locos run with three sheds down there' – which had recently been damaged by German bombing.

When the war came to an end the women were asked to relinquish their posts, to give the work to returning servicemen. Edna and Katy Nash both gave up their jobs on the buses, although Katy Nash was back in the driver's seat by the 1950s. Ruby Edwards from Whitecross, Hereford had become a porter guard on the railways, delivering parcels and freight across the country with the Great Western Railway and

London Midlands Service. 'We had to come off the railways when the men came back and I went to work at Chadds as a chargehand [supervisor] fitter.'

There was one other form of essential transport in wartime: the bicycle. 'Your bike was your friend then; you could not go anywhere unless you got your bike,' recalled John Thacker who left London in September 1942 to work on a farm near Bromyard. His bike, a Raleigh Sports had cost £6/5s before the war. 'I brought my bike. I rode to Luton Station, put it in the guards van there, then into London, rode across to Paddington Station, into the guards van again to Worcester, change to Bromyard then rode into the farm.' Cyclists covered spectacular distances. One of John's friends, John Yarnold, was courting a girl called Molly Smith who lived at Stoke Lacy. 'He used to ride all the way over there, then back to Tenbury Broad Heath ready to start work at the 'War Ag' at seven in the morning.'

John did his own courting by bicycle. He and his girlfriend Shirley would ride their bikes to distant village dances. 'The last time we rode our bikes was going to a dance at John Moore's hop farm at Shelsley Beauchamp. Coming back, Shirley got a puncture and I had to push the two bikes seven miles home.'

Scudamore schoolboy Harry Carroll worked as a Saturday errand boy for Sugarkings in Eign Gate delivering groceries and, on Saturdays, parcels to people catching their buses home. With one of his brothers training as a wireless operator and air gunner at RAF Madley, his family home was often crowded with bikes: 'When his mates had leave, they cycled to our house and left the bikes in our garden, picking them up when

Wasted wheat: initially held at a prisoner of war camp near Ledbury, Manfred 'Freddie' Kocksch was later moved to Ullingswick camp. From here he would cycle to and from the farms where he worked, often bringing back an illicit bag of wheat for bread-making. That was until he lost both bag and bike in a crash. When war ended, Freddie applied to stay in Britain, his former home having been swallowed up by East Germany. Freddie settled in Pencombe and remained here with his wife Eileen for the rest of his life. POW camp interior, drawn by Freddie Kocksch. (*Fieldwork/ The Rural Media Company*)

they returned and cycling back to Madley. They were big Air Force issue bikes: no one got the same bike that they came with.'

Occasionally there were insufficient bikes to go round. Elizabeth Godsell's bike disappeared while she was working at Redhill Hostel in 1943: 'The RAF lads had my bike: they used to steal bicycles to get back to camp after the Hostel dances.' Resourceful Italian prisoners of war encamped at Callow went into bicycle production: 'They made bikes out of bits and pieces of scrap and rode them bicycles to the bottom of Dinedor Hill to meet their friends,' recalled Henry Moss. 'They were not allowed any closer to Hereford.'

The Italians had been put to work on felling trees. Geordie Joan Foggin, who had come to Hereford to work in the Timber Corps and was quartered near Stirling Lines, had the job of selecting trees for felling. Her son Ian Robinson related how she would report to the POW camp and meet up with the Italians who were driven to the woods by lorry. Joan was expected to follow on her push-bike. 'In reality Mum waited for the lorry to round the nearest corner, when her bike went into the back of the lorry and she climbed into the cab. After the war she was sent a pair of Italian silk stockings. There was no forwarding address.'

German prisoner of war Manfred 'Freddie' Kocksch from Ullingswick managed to destroy his bike. When they were helping with the harvest he and his mates were in the habit of 'conserving' a little wheat for themselves. Under the benign eye of the camp guards the wheat was ground into flour at a local mill and baked as fresh bread back at camp. One time, however, Fred, carrying the grain on the cross bar, lost control of his bicycle. 'I went straight down this hill, across the main road and into the railings. That was the end of that bike.'

Boys and girls were adept at doubling up on a single bike, or giving each other 'backies'; although Eddie Thompson, then just nine years old, recalled sharing the family bike with his twelve-year-old brother to fetch his grandmother's medicine from Kingstone surgery. She lived six miles away at Wellbrook, Peterchurch. 'We took it in turns to ride, usually the distance between so many telegraph poles, and then on the descent of Batcho Hill we would both ride, one on the saddle, the other on the crossbar. We often failed to negotiate the sharp bend at the bottom' (Eddie's experience proved useful: he went on to compete in cyclo-cross and run a cycle business in Hereford).

As the war entered its fourth year, Sheila Hince (then Sheila Jones) from Burley Gate was pestering her parents to buy her a bike. 'My father was in the army and my mother said that I must pick hops to earn the money. I was only nine, but when hop picking finished that year I had £9.' Excited, she and her mother chose a cycle from Watsons in Commercial Road. The cycle cost £10. 'Mum gave me the extra £1. The bicycle was too large for me and the cycle shop put wooden blocks on the pedals so that I could reach them and cycle the eight miles home.'

The new bicycle was a Victory. 'It prompted Mum to remark, "I hope that the war will soon be over and we will have victory."' The war in Europe ended the following year.

8 On the Post

LETTERS FROM LOVED ONES, PARCELS FROM FRIENDS, AND TELEGRAMS BRINGING the worst news possible were as much part of the daily routine as food queues and khaki. Mary Morris, 14 years old at the time and working at the Ritz Café in Commercial Road, Hereford, recalled the fateful telegram delivered to her mother early in the war. A cook with the King's Shropshire Light Infantry (KSLI), her father had been among the first to go to war. 'He was killed in a cellar at Arnhem. His death left mum to bring seven of us up at College Estate on 32 shillings a week.'

Charlie Evans saw plenty of post pass through his hands. A teenager when war began, Charlie was following in his father's and grandfather's footsteps when he joined the post office. 'I took the Civil Service exam and went to work at RAF Credenhill at what was Stretton Sugwas Post Office.'

His father Ernie, meanwhile, was running the busy post office at Mansel Lacy, having taken over from his own father in 1919. Ernie and his wife Emily spent the war processing the mounds of mail from the Canadian soldiers, prisoners of war, wounded American GIs and Polish refugees who lived nearby at Foxley Camp (*see 'Foxley Camp', page 143*). Mansel Lacy Post Office was their contact point with the outside world.

'The Canadians were the first to move in,' recalled Charlie. 'They brought a load of timber and built a camp at the top end of Foxley. After the Canadians went, a dollop of German prisoners of war were up

Fateful news: Mary Morris, then a 14-year-old working at the Ritz Café in Hereford, learned of her father's death when a telegram arrived at the house. A cook with the Herefordshire Regiment King's Shropshire Light Infantry, he was killed at Arnhem. 'When he joined the Territorials they were the first to go into the war,' recalled Mary. 'Afterwards mum had to bring us children up on 32 shillings a week.' (*Mary Morris*)

there. They weren't here very long and they must have been trusted because there was no ring-fence.'

During the build up to the D-Day landings of July 1944, the county was flooded with American servicemen. Henry Moss remembered 'a massive American convoy with tanks and their carriers' winding up past Aconbury, heading towards the Callow prior to the invasion of France (the searchlight on top of Callow Hill was, he thought, operated by the American forces because of the concentration of U.S. army troops in the area). Joan Foggin remembered how, on the morning of D-Day, the thousands of Americans had disappeared, 'just like the May Fair slips away in the night'. In anticipation of the return of men wounded during the landings, a U.S. Army hospital, the 123rd General Hospital, was established at Foxley with two medical units under commanding officer Colonel Frank McDonald and executive officer Martin Cherkasky.

Ernie Evans, meanwhile, was a busy man, and not only through managing the mail for different forces that made Foxley their temporary home. Ernie was also the village wheelwright, carpenter and blacksmith, and acted as the local dealer for petrol and oil. His carpentry skills gave him the contract to provide coffins, and assist with the burials of any of the German prisoners of war who died at the camp. His close contacts with Foxley led to friendships, and a particularly close bond developed between him and a Canadian sapper, Bob Knowles. Bob became a regular visitor to Emily's kitchen. It led Bob's mother, Mrs John Firstbrook (she had remarried) to write and thank Ernie and Emily for looking after her son. In one letter, dated 8 November 1941, she wrote from 55 Foxbar Road, Toronto:

> Dear Mr and Mrs Evans, I am sending a bit of Xmas cake, tea and sugar. Robert enjoyed so much his little visit with you and said it was almost like going home. The people of Mansel Lacy seemed so glad to see him. Again I want to thank both of you for your kindness to my son.

Ernie's son Charlie treasured the letter, along with a scribbled note that was delivered early one Sunday morning to Ernie. It hinted at some wild revelries the previous evening and was signed by Bob:

> I don't think anything serious will come out of our trip to the village Saturday night. We came right back here and were waiting when Weinflach[?] returned. Just say you can't remember for sure. You see a lot of soldiers around and get their names mixed up a lot.

Bob then added, as an afterthought, 'Ask Mrs Evans if she can get the rabbits over please. Bob.'

Foxley friends: Sapper Bob Knowles (*crouching lower right*) with his adopted family, Ernie and Emily Evans (*left*), and a neighbour (*centre*) with Charlie Evans and his older brother Edward. Their sister Annetta, nicknamed 'Tiny', is in front. 'There seems no end to these troubles,' wrote the soldier's mother to Charlie's family. A month later Bob was dead. (*Charlie Evans*)

The rabbit pies and Saturday nights out came to an end when Bob Knowles' posting arrived. His mother wrote: '[Bob] has been away a year and a half now and it seems as if there is no end to these troubles.' The troubles soon overtook Bob: he was killed on 11 December and buried later at Brookwood Military Cemetery.

Just as Bob had found comfort and companionship at Mansel Lacy, the wounded GIs arriving back in England after the successful invasion of France were rested by their stay in the county. Leon Standifer from Baton Rouge, Louisiana gave an account of his own experiences:

> In February 1945 I was convalescing in the U.S. Army hospital located at Foxley. Physically I was recovering from wounds, frozen feet and pneumonia. Emotionally I was shattered and despondent. I was a badly frightened and shocked boy – not really a man. I had seen too much of war.

People would stop the shy young GI in uniform as he wandered through Hereford:

> I remember walking along the narrow residential streets and meeting old ladies who would stop and talk to me.
> - "It's such a lovely day."
> - "I think spring is the best time to be in Hereford."
> - "You seem to be walking better than you were last week."
> Small boys playing in their yards would ask: "Hello Yank. Any gum for us?"
> I remember a park along the Wye where I could lie and think of … absolutely nothing. One day I was lying there when a very proper little boy said: "My parents say that it's rude to ask Americans for gum, so I don't."

Entertainments were laid on for the troops:

> I remember the cinema, fish and chips, and movies ending with everyone standing to sing *God Save The King*. I remember weekly dances at the community centre [probably Redhill Hostel] where soldiers from many countries met British girls, and the girls trying, very bravely, to teach me dance steps. I didn't know how to dance and was too clumsy to learn easily. I remember some ATS girls and their British and Canadian boyfriends persuading me to try drinking local cider. I learned to enjoy it, but didn't care for the beer. I remember being embarrassed at the proper ATS girls joining us in singing *Roll Me Over*.

Writing home: Injured GI Leon Standifer *(standing, with colleague Ed O'Rourke back home in Louisiana)* convalesced at Foxley U.S. army hospital. 'I was a badly frightened boy who had seen too much of war.' *(Marie Standifer)*

Most poignant of all to the boy from Baton Rouge was the popular and patriotic classic song performed by the Forces' sweetheart, Vera Lynn: 'I remember crying when we sang: *There'll Always Be An England*.'

9 Nursing

T HE INJURED GI LEON STANDIFER REMEMBERED HEREFORDSHIRE PEOPLE FOR their 'love, warmth and tolerance – Herefordshire provided the healing love which I so desperately needed.' The war saw many different places of healing spring up around the county. Both the city hospitals and the cottage hospitals in Kington, Ross, Leominster, Ledbury and Bromyard were on high alert. There were additional U.S. army hospitals at Barons Cross in Leominster and Kington Camp on the Hergest road. The Barons Cross unit (like Foxley, set up to care for casualties from Europe) was established by the 76th U.S. General Hospital in March 1944. Their first patients were paratroopers wounded during the Normandy invasion; and when, in July, the 76th left to set up a hospital on the Continent, the 135th at Foxley took over the facility, running it until the war ended. Kington was the base for the 107th and 102nd U.S. Hospitals. A remarkable piece of colour film, shot by Corporal Clarke Morgan and now held by the Imperial War Museum, shows convoys of American ambulances pulling up at the camp, and recuperating GIs wandering through High Town.

However, the sight of the wounded soldiers arriving in the county shocked local people. 'An ambulance train drew into platform three of Barr's Court station with its

Holme Lacy Hospital: Margaret Davies (*left*) with Wren friend Francis Chant in High Town, Hereford. Margaret nursed at Holme Lacy Hospital, which had opened in the 1930s as a women's psychiatric hospital. The county hospitals were all pressed into service to help the war wounded. (*John Davies*)

distinctive khaki livery and bold Red Cross insignia,' remembered Michael Young, by then nine years old. He watched with his parents and neighbours as the wounded servicemen disembarked to take a little exercise. 'I could tell from the way my parents spoke that this was a serious occasion.'

Barbara Dawson was from a military family. The daughter of Staff Sergeant Bill Pullinger (the King's Shropshire Light Infantry man had served in the First World War and been taken prisoner of war), she lived at the Drill Hall House in Friar Street ('I always went to sleep at night to the sound of the military band playing underneath my bedroom window') until her father, now army recruiting officer, was moved with his family to live at the Bradbury Lines army camp. 'We had to black-out our windows, have an Anderson air raid shelter in the garden and manage without street lamps. There was butter and sugar on Mondays only, due to rationing, and at one time we had 11 people living in our semi.'

The neighbouring army camp served a range of purposes, 'Boys Battery, RASC [Royal Army Service Corps] and convalescent camp.' But Barbara was horrified when, going out to play one morning, she found the whole of Hoarwithy Road lined with injured men. 'They were lying in the hedges, waiting to go into the Camp. It was an awful sight. Some had legs shot off, arms missing, eyes blindfolded, head injuries, feet or hands gone. They were dressed in blue felt jackets and trousers and they were all only young.'

Wounded soldiers: Michael Young joined the RAF during National Service after the war, but as a nine-year-old he had watched an ambulance train draw into Barr's Court station across the road from where he and his family lived. As his family and neighbours looked on, he sensed the seriousness of the occasion. (*Michael Young*)

Barbara and her friend Gwen [Lock] Watkins sat with the men all that day, passing them cakes, sandwiches and drinks made by their mothers. 'There were some not so badly injured Americans amongst them who taught us to jitterbug in the middle of Hoarwithy Road.' It was a strange scene and one that remained with Barbara long after the war. 'I joined the Girls Training Corps and stayed connected with khaki all my life, but my experience with the injured troops taught me to smile even in the face of tragic times.'

Hannah Leary, a St John's nursing sister took it upon herself to assist the troops returning from Dunkirk. Her daughter Katie Causer recalled how Hannah earned the nickname 'Sister Hannah' after setting up a tea stall for the troops (she was anxiously awaiting news

Friends overseas: school girl Maureen Beauchamp with Indian soldiers stationed near Wormelow before the D-Day landings. Hannah Causer befriended several of the Indian troops camped out on Hereford racecourse. (*Maureen Beauchamp/ Derek Foxton*)

of her own son). Hannah also befriended several Indian troops. 'Widemarsh Common was covered in tents, possibly in readiness for the D-Day Landings,' recalled Katie. Hannah felt especially sorry for the Indians who had to march to the Black Mountains and back on training exercises; and one day, to show their gratitude, they made her a guest of honour at a simple ceremony in one of the tents, borrowing one of Hannah's potted plants to decorate the tent.

Nurses like Margery Dale (later Burman) of Huntley, Preston-on-Wye, lived in, or close to, their hospitals so that they could be on ward at a moment's notice. 'It was so very busy when we had casualties over from France. You lived in the hospital. The wounded left France about four o'clock in the afternoon and arrived with us in the early hours of the morning. We [would be] on duty all the time.'

Too busy: Margery Dale (*above: second from left, immaculately turned out; and left: back row, far right, in midwifery guise*). 'During air raids we were supposed to go to the shelters – I never did: we were far too busy.' (*Mo Burns*)

Margery had trained as a nurse in 1939, moving into midwifery at Leeds after four years basic training in Worcester. The journey from Worcester to her family home at Huntley in Preston-on-Wye was too long to be undertaken often: 'I did get home sometimes, but there was no petrol in those days, so I'd get a bus as far as Bridge Sollars and [wait for someone] to fetch me.'

Leeds brought new challenges – 'there were a lot of Jewish patients and we had to be careful with their diets' – and Margery rarely left the hospital:

> For months we were not allowed to go beyond a five-mile radius in case we had to be called back quickly. During air raids we were supposed to go down to the shelters – somehow I never did. We were far too busy to bother about anything else, so I stayed in bed.

Margery left nursing to marry a wounded serviceman who had suffered 40% burns and two smashed knees. He was the only survivor of a motor torpedo boat which had been blown up in the Mediterranean.

Many men came to Herefordshire for convalescence. Garnstone Castle near Weobley was turned into a nursing home, as was Wessington Court at Woolhope, owned by Mr Bond, director of Evans Cider Works on Widemarsh Common. This became a convalescent hospital for wounded soldiers, mainly from the Scots Regiments. The men came to rely on head-gardener Bill Jones' many skills, as his daughter June Smith, then seven, recalled. 'When the ambulance arrived, father would help unload and settle the men in their wards before giving each a haircut – they said it made them feel human again.' He laid on fresh fruit and vegetables from the gardens, and rearranged the main hall into a little cinema for the once-a-month visit from the Mobile Picture Unit. *Pathé News* followed by a comedy and the main feature film were screened on a sheet draped over the Court staircase. 'There was a special chair in front for me, wheelchairs behind and bedridden patients at the back,' remembered June. On some nights the drone of bomber engines sounded overhead: 'They were nervous moments – the greenhouses must have looked like water from above.' June was convinced the family dog could distinguish between friendly and foreign planes, 'wagging his tail at ours and growling at the Germans'.

Broadlands, on Aylestone Hill in Hereford, eventually used to house student teachers from the training college, was temporarily pressed into service as another convalescent home. The injured residents were mainly Scandinavian troops, and a request was put out to the city's switchboard operators, judged to have the best and clearest English speaking voices, to drop by and entertain the troops. The men expressed their gratitude to the well-spoken women by presenting them with a signed painting.

Most injured servicemen expected to return to the fray, and they made the most of their time in Herefordshire. At Wessington the 'Jocks' walked June to and from school and wandered around the gardens. One remained in the county, marrying a local girl

Sixth sense: 'Our dog could tell the difference between ours' and the enemy planes flying overhead,' recalled June Smith. Her father Bill was head gardener at Wessington Court, Woolhope, which lay on the bombers' flight path. The Court, home to Evans Cider Works director Mr Bond, served as one of the county's many convalescent homes for wounded soldiers. (*June Smith*)

and finding a job at Marks and Spencer. 'There was also a Belgian, rescued on the beach at Dunkirk, who spoke no English when he arrived. He left fluent, but with a strong Scots accent,' June remembered. 'I wonder how many of those boys came through the war. It was a tough time.'

If the war wounded needed care, the civilians had health needs of their own. Tupsley's isolation hospital was filled to capacity by an outbreak of diphtheria and scarlet fever at Hunderton in 1939. One child, Dorothy King of Catherine Street, died. Another of the sick children, Peter Morris, remembered being tended by the matron, Jones, 'always dressed in a grey uniform'. He was attended to by two nurses, Hilda Price and Nurse Parker and the ambulance man who lived in a cottage on the drive. This was former First World War submariner Harold Vaughan who ran a horse-drawn ambulance for patients and a larger van which he used to fetch clothes and bedding from infected houses to be disinfected at the hospital. His daughter, Joyce Densham, recalled the typhoid hospital that stood a couple of fields away.

Free health care was still unavailable. One Hereford mother called the doctor because she was afraid her five-year-old daughter was seriously ill. 'I rang him and said: "Well I think she's got pneumonia", and he said: "What do you know about pneumonia? I can't come out to charity cases," the old bugger said to me.'

With her husband Joe fighting in Italy, she could do no more than nurse her child through the night. The hospitals were full of wounded service people and there was no Penicillin to be had:

> She died on the Monday morning and he [the doctor] came. I cursed him. I nearly kicked him down the stairs. I said: "You should have come. You could have saved her life."
>
> I said to him: "Well don't you ever send a bill for me," I said, "because I'll never, never pay it."
>
> He never sent me a bill. They tried to get Joe home, but he was in the front line. He couldn't get back. She'd been buried a month when he came home.

Women who joined the forces could expect some degree of health screening, although munitions worker Adelaide Weekes concluded that the medicals were pretty cursory. She did not enjoy receiving hers for ROF Rotherwas: 'Everybody had to strip off to their waist: I didn't like that very much'. Having passed fit, Adelaide settled to work alongside a young girl from Kington. 'I got very pally with Nell – a short, well-built girl who was also looking after her sick mother. We used to have a warm-up in the winter, standing against the radiators before the charge hand called you to your line.'

One morning Nell seemed unable to rise from her bench. Adelaide told their charge hand, Sylvia, who sent the pair to the works' surgery. Adelaide left Nell with the nurses, returning to her bench to cover for Nell until her lunch break. Then she walked to the surgery to check on her friend.

'When I got there this nurse went mad at me. She said: "your friend wasn't fit to walk up here". I didn't know, but Nell had had a baby on the way – you didn't know anything about sex: we were all so innocent in those days.' The baby was delivered as Nell was rushed to hospital. Adelaide went to visit her that night. 'I went down the General to see her, but she was in an isolation ward because she had puerperal fever.' She returned the following Saturday only to discover that Nell had died. 'She must have had that baby within a month of her medical. Now what sort of medical was it?'

Doing her bit. Connie Williams started work at Hereford's Food Office in 1939. 'Having been in the Hereford Territorial Army at camp in Weston-super-Mare my husband was therefore in the Army from then on. How would I manage on the money? I went to the Labour Exchange, asked about a job and got an interview for a post in the Food Office. I started there on the first Monday in October. We used the Town Hall's Main Hall (a big change from the dances that used to be held there). There was no overtime pay in those first months and I often had to work late, as the Town Clerk was also Fuel Officer, Billeting Officer, etc. But I didn't mind as I thought I was doing my bit for my country to help win the war.' (*Connie Williams*)

Aside from war wounds and medical shortages most people were said to be healthier than ever. With sugar and fat rationed, meat in short supply, and everyone forced to take exercise, few were burdened by excess weight. The truth, recalled fighter pilot Brian Davies, was not quite so simple. 'You never saw anyone fat, particularly in the services, because of their physical fitness. But you were on a restricted amount of food and you either went around moaning that you were starving … or you had another cigarette. Because everyone smoked in those days.' Stan Fryer, the young lad working the buses out of Llangarron, agreed: 'Lots of people smoked or did snuff.'

10 Redhill Hostel

THE HALLS AND ROOMS AT REDHILL HOSTEL WERE PERMANENTLY WREATHED IN tobacco smoke. The Hostel, a cross between a barracks and Butlins holiday camp, stood on the Ross Road. It was home to thousands of war workers, Land Army girls, the Women's Timber Corps, construction workers, transport drivers ferrying essential supplies to the ports before and after D-Day, refugees from Europe, railwaymen and student teachers.

Railway men: many Hereford railwaymen were housed at Redhill Hostel along with munitions workers and women from the Land Army. (*Back, left to right*): Les Twissle, Derick Davies, Dilwyn Davis, Jimmy Talbot, John 'the Pole', Sid Ead, Morris Jones, 'Bomber' Roberts. (*Centre*) Walter Lake, Edgar Jones, Walter Donovan, Alan Bowden, Alan Evans, John Davies, Dai Lewis, Sam Wilby, Alan Roberts, unknown, Bill Yoxal, Glyn Roberts. (*Front*) Maldwyn Davies, Stan East, Reg Hodges, Hostel worker Miss Reynolds, Horace Broad, Hostel worker Miss Bartlett, Ron Preece, unknown and Norman Crokom. (*John Davies*)

Built by the Ministry of Supply in 1941, Redhill could accommodate nearly 2,000 residents, although numbers averaged 1,250 at any one time. About 120 staff were employed, mostly as 'bedroom stewards' (chamber maids) in the 20, single-storey sleeping blocks and as dining room staff. Two cavernous dining halls could each cater for 500 at one sitting. There was a large concert hall and plays were put on featuring West End stars such as John Clements, Googie Withers, Sybil Thorndike and Sonia Dresdel. One resident recalled practising ballet leaps with her friends after a rare and inspiring visit by Ballet Rambert. There was a residents' lounge, sick bay and chapel. Telephonists, including Pat Duffield from Whitecross Road, maintained a three-shift, round-the-clock service on the Hostel switchboard.

Regarded as a national showpiece, the Hostel was run by the Holiday Fellowship Company, which had operated country guest houses before the war. Land Girl Prinia Prior described it as 'more like a classy Butlins – although,' she admitted, 'I had never been to one.' (Billy Butlins was rumoured to have played a role in its design). Prinia Prior lodged at the Hostel:

Larking around: Elizabeth Godsell of Woolhope (*centre*) and friends Vera and Lil entertained their friends with a mock wedding at Redhill Hostel. The Hostel employed 120 staff including Elizabeth, Vera and Lil: 'We'd retire to our hard, little bunks after our nine-hour shifts and fall fast asleep.' (*Elizabeth Godsell*)

The camp was composed of dozens of long, sleeping quarters with two bunks to a room; each section with its own boot room (sitting room) and drying room. There was a splendid dance hall which doubled as a cinema and theatre, a lounge, writing and reading room, and huge dining halls where we got very good food.

Most of the Holiday Fellowship's houses had been requisitioned for war work, and their surplus of trained catering staff were drafted in to serve at Redhill alongside local recruits, including Elizabeth Godsell from Woolhope.

Elizabeth put in nine-hour shifts in the dining hall. 'Early shift one week; late shift the next. It was very hard work and we retired to our hard little bunks and fell fast asleep.' All staff worked a seven-day week, the eighth being a rest-day, with a week-end off every six weeks. 'There was no choice of a meal: if you didn't like it you had to go without. But you always had a cooked breakfast which included sausages.' Among the various residents enjoying their breakfast sausages (Elizabeth referred to them as 'widows' memories') were 74 students from the teacher training college. Unlike the munitions workers who were expected to share a room, teaching-students like Marjorie Freeman (later Marjorie Crump) had a room to herself on Block D (Block D was reserved for the students, and managed by 'a dragon of a warden to keep an eye on us,' recalled trainee teacher Anne Fox).

Marjorie highlighted one problem with the accommodation: 'Being on ground level meant that we could find strange men trying to get into our rooms should we leave a window open at night.' Her room measured 10 feet by 6 feet, and was furnished with a wash basin, government utility chest of drawers, wardrobe, folding table, upright chair, armchair and – a comparative luxury for many – a radiator ('no more chilblains,' noted a grateful Marjorie). The wooden bunk-bed, drilled for ventilation, was fitted with a two-inch thick horsehair mattress. Bathrooms stood at one end of the corridors, and there was a small communal sitting room equipped with an electric kettle at the other. Meals, taken in a hanger-like dining room, 'were more varied, if less elegantly served, than those at college' – and dances held in the recreation areas attracted RAF servicemen who, noted Marjorie with dismay, were 'not nearly so handsome in their civvies.'

The student teachers travelled to college on a special bus scheduled to leave in time for them to attend college prayers at 8.30 a.m. They returned at night, often looking forward to the rich social mix that Redhill offered. Anne Fox found herself lodging with folks 'from all walks of life, but chiefly war workers who were at the munitions factory down the road.' The many migrants and refugees, displaced by the fighting in Europe, made an impression on her: 'Among the residents were men who had escaped from occupied countries: I remember one in particular who mixed HP sauce with his porridge at breakfast.'

John Hunt joined the administrative staff at Redhill working in what he described as 'an Aladdin's Cave of food and fags', the YMCA Western Stores Depot at No. 6 St Owen's Street:

> This housed all sorts of goodies only faintly remembered in the rationed world outside. Tinned fruit and jam, sacks of sugar, hundreds of biscuit tins, thousands of cigarettes and chocolate bars were among the goods stored at No. 6 with its wide side entrance. The goods would have commanded a high price on the black market, and yet there was never any attempted break-in or theft.

The Hereford YMCA served military camps where there was no NAAFI, as well as gun sites and Land Army hostels. Many of the goods arrived on a weekly van delivery load from Carmarthen. John had been based in Carmarthen until 1942 when he was transferred to No. 6 St Owen Street to become its storekeeper.

'Goods flowed in and flowed out again like a tide. I had as sole assistant an elderly man, Bert, who'd been bombed-out in Birmingham. Together, day after day, we lugged goods, including 140lb sugar sacks, from delivery lorries into the yard.' They grew to dread one particular delivery: biscuits.

> We grew to hate the 7lb biscuit tins, sometimes up to 120 in a consignment, which had to be carted all the way to the upper rooms where they were stacked ceiling high. All eventually had to come down again. I have never felt the same about biscuits since carrying them, six at a time up the stairs, only to see them come down again a week later.

John was eventually beaten by the tide of biscuits: 'Fed up with broken finger nails, bruises and a back strained from carrying sugar sacks, I applied for an administrative post on the staff at Redhill late in 1942, and the Aladdin's Cave at No. 6 saw the last of me.'

Joan Thomas, the Shropshire policeman's daughter who had left home to join the Timber Corps, arrived at the Hostel fresh-faced and ready for work:

> The Hostel was a new world with its glassed-in reception area. A very efficient man with the most attractive voice dealt with us quickly (too quickly for me, as I liked the look of him). I summed him up on the spot: intelligent – the spectacles bore testimony to that; below average height – *oh, but I can wear my flatties*. I had almost fixed our wedding date. He was smartly dressed – *but then I've brought my navy two-piece with the white trim, and my flatties are navy too so it'll be all right*. He dispatched us with our keys and a typed list of dos and don'ts without giving me a second glance.

Joan was intrigued by the Hostel's reading and writing rooms, ('we could buy writing paper, envelopes and stamps from reception'), its cute little library, the residents' lounge 'with a radio and luxurious armchairs grand enough for any hotel', and a social office equipped with sports equipment which residents could borrow.

The large, maple-floored dance hall with its stage and dressing rooms was cleaned by Eric Caton. He had a tiny, grizzled face, deep-set eyes, a wicked grin and a string of filthy stories. He'd worked in a circus looking after the lions. He was proud of his affinity with his lions. No doubt they'd heard his filthy stories first.

The social calendar was managed by a portly social director, Eric Newall. 'He looked every inch the West End theatre manager. He had been a railway booking clerk before the war and his favourite reading when on a lavatory seat was rumoured to be Bradshaw's Railway Timetable.'

Joan judged the entertainment to be 'fab':

There were Entertainments National Service Association (ENSA or 'Every Night Something Awful') and Council for the Encouragement of Music and the Arts (CEMA) shows, while film and stage stars Googie Withers and her husband John McCallum played alongside each other in a stage production of *They Came to a City*.

Hostel romance: evacuated from London, Joyce Fromings was eventually housed at Redhill Hostel along with hundreds of women who, like her, worked at Royal Ordnance Factory Rotherwas. She would marry Eric Lambert, another munitions worker, seen here alongside Eric's best man and his factory boss, Tony Casatelli. (*John Lambert*)

The author, J.B. Priestley, gave a cameo performance. 'A Negro Ballet Company brought us a wonderful stage performance, and we had entertainers such as Bernard Miles ("Best bit of sharpin' stone in 'ertford-shire"). The pattern of operation for Redhill Hostel was, like the famous Windmill Theatre motto: "We Never Close."'

With such a rich mix of residents, the occasional romance was inevitable. One of the railway workers housed at Redhill was Horace Broad. The 38-year-old from Shenmore met and married Dorothy Morgan, an examiner at ROF Rotherwas, at Redhill.

Bromley-born Joyce Fromings had been evacuated from London – first to Kinnersley and later, when she started work at ROF Rotherwas, to the Hostel. She married Eric Lambert (a progress chaser at the munitions laboratory) who had worked there in the First World War. Eric's boss, and their best man, was Tony Casatelli, remembered as the man whose unambiguous instructions for loading shells allowed almost anyone to work the 25-pounder line.

Redhill resident: Winston and Vera Oakley had met at the munitions factory where they both worked. (*Vera Oakley*)

Munitions worker Vera Lewis had been living on her father William Lewis' farm at Allensmore when she got a job filling empty shells with TNT explosive at the munitions factory:

> I met a young forklift truck driver, Winston Clive Oakley from the Forest of Dean who was staying at Redhill Hostel. His nickname was 'Curly'. Mine was 'Ginge'. At the shift's end [at Rotherwas] he would help me stack the many boxes. I worked four years at the factory and later Clive and I married and went on to have our children: John, Marilyn, Beryl, Irene and Carol.

11 Evacuees

THE FIRST EVACUEES ARRIVED AT HEREFORDSHIRE'S TRAIN STATIONS EARLY IN 1940. The *Hereford Times* anticipated the arrival of 700 children, prompting letters from concerned readers worried about the health, hygiene and possible behaviour of these lost city kids. When the expected bombing of British cities failed to take place, far fewer children were put on the trains to Hereford. Many of those who did come were sent to surrounding villages. At Castle Frome a few evacuees, mostly from Birmingham, were billeted around the parish. They attended the village school, their numbers squeezing the timetable and causing the children's attendances to be reduced to half-days. At neighbouring Bishops Frome, school space in the classroom was already at a premium. Harry Carroll's family had moved here from London and because his parents were both out on land work he took his little brother to school. 'He couldn't have been more than three and he'd stand by my desk while I did my schoolwork.' That September, 119 children and their teachers were evacuated from Birmingham and placed in St Martins School, Belmont, trebling the school roll under headmistress Fanny Brook.

The girls of St Francis Xavier's Catholic School in Berrington Street had encountered evacuees two years earlier. One girl, Monica Williams, remembered her class teacher warning them to be nice to a group of new arrivals: 'We went out to play and there they were: dark eyes, dark hair.' The mysterious newcomers were Basque children fleeing the Spanish Civil War of 1937. That May almost 4,000 Republican children, escaping the Nationalist air raids, assisted by German Luftwaffe pilots honing their *Blitzkrieg* techniques, left on the *Expedición a Inglaterra*, the English Expedition, aboard a ship, the SS *Habana*, bound for Southampton. One group was accompanied by its teacher and guardian, a 22-year-old Catalan called Josefina Carmen. They were accommodated by the Sisters of Charity at Lower Bullingham and sent to school at St Francis. 'Some of the bigger girls taught us a skipping game,' recalled Monica: "'*Istaba, laba rerra, frandi, frandango, nebagay, nebagando, frandu, frandango*".' Joan Clements, another of the St Francis girls, also remembered the dark-eyed Spaniards. In her nineties she could still sing, in Latin, the *Salve Regine* the girls had taught her.

Escaping the *Blitzkrieg*: Herefordshire welcomed a group of Spanish evacuees in 1937–38. Fleeing the bombings of their Basque homes carried out by a Luftwaffe Unit and supported by Spain's Nationalist forces, children boarded the Southampton-bound SS *Habana* and set out for England. This group was given shelter by the Sisters of Charity at Lower Bullingham along with their teacher and guardian, 22-year-old Catalan Josefina Carmen. They attended St Francis Catholic School and made Hereford their home. Once the military dictator Francisco Franco took power in Spain, many, including Josefina, would never return. (*Lita Power*)

Josefina Carmen eventually settled in Herefordshire, marrying merchant navy man Jack Jones and raising a family here, according to her daughter Lita Power in her book *Beyond the SS Habana – A Family Story*: 'Some [girls] never returned, either because their families had been killed or because relatives warned them to stay in England. And when Josefina died her tombstone at Little Birch was engraved: *Que En Paz Descanse*. May She Rest In Peace.'

As with the Spanish girls, friendships sprang up between country children and the city evacuees. Dorothy Vaughan from Ross-on-Wye became best friends with an evacuee, Maureen Harper, billeted with Maureen's brother Billy at a Mrs Gilbert's in Morley Square. She also befriended two Jewish boys from Birmingham, Alan Mychenski and David Leibovitz. Friends were important: in July 1942 Dorothy thought she had lost her mum, also called Dorothy, who worked with her two sisters Rose and Vera at Hereford's munitions factory:

> Someone came to break the news to Dad: "Sorry Billy, but your wife has been killed." Everyone was crying until Mum was spotted, coming up the road from

Ross station wearing an odd boot she had been given – she had been walking in for her morning shift when the factory came under attack (*see 'On the Munitions', page 85*). Apart from being thrown to the ground and losing a shoe she was unhurt.

Many evacuee siblings were upset and traumatised by being separated and sent to different homes. Sympathetic residents helped where they could. Dorothy recalled children sitting on pavements in Hillview and Three Crosses Road while neighbours brought out food and jugs of powdered lemonade.

When nine-year-old Pamela Double arrived with her twelve-year-old and three-year-old brothers in the summer of 1940, the two brothers were sent to Almeley while she and another girl went to Canon Pyon:

> It was so late [when we arrived] our people had gone to bed so we stayed the night in the vicarage cottage. Next day we met Mr and Mrs Lewis – they asked us to call them Uncle Will and Aunty Em. I don't think she was that pleased to have two nine-year-old girls to stay, but Uncle Will, who was the gardener at the vicarage, took to us straight away.

The reluctant 'Aunty Em' seemed to have been won over by her young guests. 'We were well treated and went to school in the village. I liked helping Will in the garden and going up to the farm to collect eggs and look after the calves. I loved the country life and stayed till Mother found a house in Hereford.' Margaret never left Hereford again.

As the war went on, Germany stepped up its air raids on British cities. More evacuees arrived in Herefordshire, including ten-year-old Mavis Owen. Like Margaret she would make Herefordshire her home after being evacuated from Liverpool in January 1941. As the first, heavy blitz hit the city, Mavis was hurried onto the evacuee train without bidding her mum goodbye:

> When we were taken to the station our mums weren't allowed on the platform in case they were too upset. The dads put us on board.
>
> I had never been so far from home and I cried bitter tears because I thought I would never see my mum and dad again. Our train took us to Llandrindod Wells and we stayed overnight in an hotel. Then we were taken to our respective lodgings. I was taken to 16, The Village, Clyro before I went on to stay with Mr and Mrs Evans at a smallholding called Paradise. The place was true to its name. I was very happy and they were kind and caring people.

Mavis passed her scholarship and went to Brobury House. 'There were ten girls there and it was like being at boarding school. Our school from Liverpool had taken over Hergest Croft in Kington and again we were very happy.' Mavis returned home to Liverpool in 1944, but the lure of country life proved unsettling: she returned three years later to join the Land Army.

Broxwood Court: the controversial wartime author J.B. Priestley with Hereford greengrocer Sid Wright. The author's house at Almeley was turned into a home for evacuee mothers and children by Priestley's wife at the time, Jane Wyndham-Lewis. The author continued to compose his national wartime broadcasts for the BBC from here until the Corporation decided he was too controversial and axed his talks. Priestley also gave a cameo performance at the Redhill Hostel. (*Michael Young*)

Twins Derek and Geoffrey Baker and their mother Peggy were bombed out of their home in London and, after a few nights sleeping on the Underground platforms at night, Peggy got in touch with the author J.B. Priestley who had a home in Herefordshire. John and Jane Priestley lived at Broxwood Court, Almeley, running their home as a hostel for bombed-out women and children, many of the children orphaned. The project was partly funded by the American Foster Parents Plan. It was from Broxwood that Priestley wrote his inspiring *Radio Postscripts*, broadcast to the nation by the BBC on Sunday nights. However, when his talks began to focus on politics and the need for better social democracy when the war was over, the BBC dropped his broadcasts. The Hereford pacifist and greengrocer, Sid Wright, was a regular visitor to Broxwood.

Peggy Baker, who had contacted Priestley through the actress Cicely Courtneidge, arranged for her twins to stay at Broxwood. 'We were there for maybe a year then moved to the old Quaker orphanage home on Rylands Hill Road in Leominster,' recalled Derek.

Geoffrey and his brother went to the pictures, keeping up with the news on *British Movietone* and *Pathé News*. There were German POWs imprisoned nearby and 'Free Poles' billeted in the town. 'We attended Brooke Hall Sunday School and we never felt scared or deprived.' At Christmas, although there were precious few presents, there was the odd surprise: a toothbrush for each of the children from the German POWs. Their kindness stemmed from an earlier encounter. 'A dozen of us had walked past the camp and the adult with us [had] stopped to chat with one of the Germans. That German toothbrush wasn't much by worldly standards, but the sentiment has stuck with me for years. This was a very happy time.' Derek's and Geoffrey's mother Peggy, meanwhile, having worked at one of the American medical units, now found a job at the munitions factory in Rotherwas. Another Leominster evacuee was jazz musician Johnny Dankworth who was moved to Ford Bridge in 1941.

With their mothers at work and often on fire-fighting duties at night, and their fathers away fighting or hospitalised, youngsters learned to fend for themselves – sometimes with tragic consequences, as High School boy John Slatford recalled:

> I was in my third year at the School in 1940 when Birmingham's St Philip's Grammar School brought 195 evacuee boys and 14 masters to Hereford. To accommodate the newcomers our school day ran from 9.00 a.m. until 1.00 p.m. and the Birmingham boys were there from 1.30 until 5.30 p.m.
>
> January was said to be the coldest month ever recorded in Hereford and the Wye was frozen over by the Castle Green. Having a half day free was a novelty and many children played on the river. But on the afternoon of January 18 between 40 and 50 children were playing on the ice when it gave way, plunging eight or nine children into freezing water over eight feet deep. Some scrambled to safety, but four of the children, Elva Mudge, Jocelyn Whitlock, Heather Berryman (all 12 years old and pupils at the High School for Girls), and Denis Mason from St Philips, were drowned. Survivors Decia Green, 10, was taken straight to hospital, and Iris Cotterell, 12, to the fire station in Wye Street.

In later years Decia remembered the moment the ice gave way:

> We'd been playing down by the Bassom in Bartonsham then went up river, which was completely frozen over, to where the Art College was [below the Castle Green]. Apparently a lady had committed suicide just below the school and they had broken the ice to get her out. One of the boys said: "See how far you can go", and suddenly there was this awful cracking noise and we all just went straight in.
>
> It was all green and our heavy clothes weighed us down. So many things flashed in my head including my father saying: "Don't go near the river." I came up and there was a Chinese girl from our school whose father ran the laundry opposite Ogilvy's where the RAF men used to get their collars done. "Audrey! Audrey!" I shouted. "Come and save me!" I went down again, came back up again and Audrey was saying something but I couldn't hear. I don't remember any more.

At the inquest into the deaths of the four children the coroner commended the efforts of rescuers, Hereford Training College student Margaret James, Roma Dean from Bridge Street, Francis Collins of Stanhope Street and Henry Cairns of Baysham Street.

A little more than a term later St Philip's returned home, influenced perhaps by the river tragedy.

It became increasingly difficult for the authorities and welfare agencies to meet the needs of neglected children. Birmingham-born Eileen Buckley had found herself stranded in Hereford at the end of a family holiday in 1939, her parents too fearful to take her home. She was put with a family friend, and later her grandmother who had been bombed out of Birmingham:

I'd made friends with a girl and one day we climbed a ladder into this old building, to look round, but when we went to go back, someone had removed the ladder. Panic! It was too far to jump down. Finally we called out to a couple of 15-year-old boys and one of them climbed a drainpipe by the wall, got through a window where we were standing, and helped us out and down the drainpipe. We were a bit dirty and scratched but safe.

Weathering the emotional storms of childhood was something children normally shared with their parents. Eileen, deprived of her parents and living with the family friend and her daughter, became deeply unhappy:

I was always writing to my Mother to let me come home. Saturday afternoons Uncle would take us 'up the Canny', the local brook where I'd go along a tree branch that hung over the water as far as I could without getting my feet wet. Uncle turned a blind eye, but my 'cousin' told on me and I was in trouble.

Starting school at St Francis Xavier, Eileen found the nuns kind and, not being a Catholic, she was permitted to say her own prayers in private. 'The prayers consisted of hoping my parents and brother (ten years older and a navigator in the RAF) were safe'. As her first wartime Christmas approached, her mum promised to send her a railway ticket home – Birmingham had still suffered no air raids – but when, by Christmas Eve, the ticket failed to materialise, Eileen packed a suitcase and walked out into the night. 'I got as far as my favourite tree down the Canny and sat there sobbing. My uncle found me and brought me back to the house.'

While there were no presents for Eileen on the following Christmas morning, there was a surprise. 'There was a knock at the front door and there stood my father come to take me home. Wonderful!'

Life did not become any easier for the ten-year-old. She returned to Hereford after Christmas with her Mum who, after a heated argument with 'Aunty', put her to stay with another family member and her grandmother – she had been bombed out of Birmingham – in a flat on the College estate. The flat was so small Eileen had to sleep on a sofa, her grandmother in a chair. By the age of 11 she had moved to Bluecoat School, riding to classes on her bicycle. One morning the city girl was confronted by a herd of cows milling across the road as they were driven into Hereford market. 'The fellow with them said for me to go through them: no way! I was terrified.' She arrived late for school and was summoned to the headmistress'

Unhappy evacuee: Ten-year-old Eileen Buckley packed a suitcase and tried to run home to Birmingham. (*Eileen Carpenter*)

Senior evacuees: more than 50 Chelsea Pensioners were evacuated from London, many of them housed at Moraston House in Bridstow. (*Gordon Armand*)

office to explain herself. The headmistress had also encountered the herd. When Eileen blurted out: 'But you were in a car, I was on a bike', she was given ten strokes of the cane on each hand for insolence. 'I never forgave that headmistress.'

Eileen's life reached rock-bottom when her armchair-bound grandma died and she was sent to live with yet another family. Eventually, life for the little evacuee picked up. She was found a new home, a house with a large garden, and one in which she was kindly treated. Still homesick she nevertheless settled down, finding peace of mind in gardening:

> I was given a patch of garden to grow some flowers. Most of the garden was vegetables, and tomatoes were grown in two greenhouses. I was allowed to pick and weigh the tomatoes when anyone came to buy them, and I could sell some of my flowers. With the sixpence that Mom sent me each week I could save and buy presents with my own money.

Children were not the only evacuees. Retired soldiers were moved out of the Royal Hospital Chelsea to Rudhall Manor near Ross in September 1939. Moraston House in Bridstow and another house in Leighton Buzzard were also pressed into service for the 52 old soldiers, and 23 of those who died during the war would be buried at St Mary's

Betty Webb: 'The war did me no favours.' Evacuated from London, Betty lost her mother in a road accident and spent months in a hospital before finding herself marooned in Hereford, trying to find a job that would pay the rent. She ended up at the Barronia factory. (*Betty Webb*)

churchyard in Ross. Freda Morris, meanwhile, witnessed some very different evacuees settling in. 'Miss Chapman, who was known as Chapman's Circus, had animals evacuated to Acton Beauchamp Rectory. We used to go down to the Rectory to see the animals being trained.'

Many evacuees adapted to their new hosts and unfamiliar surroundings, and coped well enough with the temporary loss of their families. Yet for others the war destroyed everything they held dear – parents, home, school and surroundings. For some, evacuation turned into a trauma that they never spoke about.

North Londoner Betty Webb was 11 when war was declared. She did not choose to share her experiences as an evacuee until she turned 90. As she put it: 'War did me no favours.' Betty had started at her London high school in 1939, when the school was evacuated to the Midlands. She boarded with a local family where she was pressed into domestic service. 'We hadn't been there two minutes when she [the mother] had us cleaning the brasses. She made us tie dusters on our feet [to polish the floors], but at least she fed us.'

By 1940 Betty was back in London and the Blitz had begun:

> There were guns minutes away in Regents Park, and a few streets away a whole
> street came down. A school opened for half-days in Laycock Street and we went
> there. We [children] all had linen shrapnel bags to collect the shrapnel.
>
> My brother Sidney joined the RAF – most of our street turned out to see
> him go. He became a gunner instructor.

Betty's father, Sidney Botton, worked at Mount Pleasant Post Office and, because of
the Blitz, persuaded his wife Rosina, a court dress maker, to take Betty and her older
sister, Stella, away from London. They were to set up home in a little wooden bunga-
low the family rented at Hockley on the Essex coast. 'Soon after my sister joined the
WAAFs and left to work on the barrage balloons.' Then tragedy struck. Late in 1942
Betty was travelling on a local bus with her mother through the village of Holbridge
when it was involved in a serious accident. Four people, including her mother, were
killed and Betty was rushed to hospital.

Betty suffered amnesia and only learned of her mother's death three months later.
Betty also suffered serious facial injuries, and when her treatment failed to improve –
'the local dentist had patched me up' – she was transferred to a special plastic surgery
unit at St Albans. The 15-year-old was deeply distressed by her initial encounters with
her fellow patients, mostly air crewmen who had been badly disfigured by their injuries. 'The airmen would have these pedicles: pieces of skin taken from their sides and
grafted on to a cheek or a nose. It was shocking at first, but you got used to it.' As her
treatment improved, Betty would join the injured men for tea and cakes in a local tea
shop. But she had another shock in store: when she was sufficiently recovered to return
home, her father made it clear she could no longer stay in the family home. He had
started a relationship with another woman.

'Because my brother was stationed nearby [at RAF Credenhill] I was sent to
Hereford.' The 16-year-old fought to find work and a home:

> On my first day I went to the Labour Exchange, which was in a room next to the
> Town Hall, and was sent to a couple of shops. My brother had found me tempo-
> rary digs at 11 Hopton Road and then in Barton Road. But the shops only paid
> £1/7s a week and, as the digs were £1/17s/6d, I returned to the Labour Exchange
> that afternoon and asked for a better job. "Well," said the girl, "if you're very
> good you can go down to Barronia Metals. They need someone in the office."
>
> "How much are they paying?"
>
> "£3 a week."

Betty's problems were not over yet. Her kindly Barton Road landlady reluctantly asked
her to leave – 'she said she couldn't be responsible for a 16-year-old' – and she was sent

to live with a family in Three Elms Road. 'They were awful! They'd send you to bed in the evenings. You couldn't blame them: they'd been forced to take me in.'

Betty eventually found lodgings at the new Redhill Hostel, which accommodated girls when they were seventeen and a half. 'I loved it. It was like an army camp, all divided into these little rooms.'

But Betty had one more misfortune to overcome: her marriage. 'I met someone from Barronia and married him. It was a mistake.' Looking back on her disastrous war, and now in the company of six daughters, Betty reflected on war: 'That job at Barronia saw me settled in Hereford for good. I hated it and I hated everybody. I was determined to survive just to get back at my father. But I never saw him again.' Betty was frustrated by her powerlessness as a woman. 'You were dependent on a man. For everything. And that was awful. Today, women have got everything they want. They work for it, but the opportunities are there.'

Wartime secrets: Barronia production manager C.H. 'Tony' Williams, was also involved in research into a clandestine new weapon, the jet engine. (*Maureen Beauchamp and Derek Foxton*)

12   Barronia

Barronia Metals, the company that gave Betty Webb a job and rescued her from penury, was based in a former garage in the centre of Hereford city. Its role in keeping British bombers in the air over Europe was virtually unknown for 60 years after the war. Chris Tomlinson takes up the story:

> Aircraftings or Barronia Metals manufactured aircraft fuel valves at their factory in west London. The product was critical to the war effort because every aircraft required them (particularly the Spitfire and Hurricane) and the factory workforce had been putting in a seven-day week until one Sunday in September 1940 when they were finally given the day off. That same day the Germans dropped a stick of bombs on the factory.

Although no one was killed, the factory was destroyed.

The next day the factory draughtsman, Chris's father Reg, and another employee, Tony Williams, were dispatched to Hereford with a drawing board strapped to the back of their car. The two men stayed at the Imperial Hotel in Widemarsh Street. Over breakfast one morning, the men observed a group of pigs being led down the street to market. One man turned to the other: 'If this is going to be a long war then Hereford looks to be as good a place as any'.

The pair were instructed to draw up plans for the conversion of Fryers Garage in Widemarsh Street. The garage had been requisitioned by the army, recalled Doreen Oldman who was brought up in a neighbouring house. 'We lived next door to the works which was being used as an army supply depot with 30 to 40 soldiers billeted there. My mother cooked all their meals.' Her father would shortly find work at the newly-established Barronia Metals.

In November, equipment started to be moved up from London to Hereford, along with staff. Albert West and his newly-wed wife Winnie drove up from London in their motorbike and sidecar, with the company's recent wedding gift, a carriage clock, tucked in beside Winnie. 'People knew nothing about our work,' Albert recalled.

In late 1940 the company was on the verge of making an important break-through. Chris Tomlinson again: 'The RAF was suffering a significant number of casualties from aircraft running out of fuel and crashing, despite having full reserve tanks.' It was eventually discovered that freezing temperatures at high altitude could suddenly cut off the fuel supply causing the aircraft to lose power and crash. A modified Barronia fuel valve solved the problem. Without knowing it, many aircrews owed their lives to the Barronia fuel valve.

Despite being the head designer at Barronia, Reg Tomlinson would travel to work every day from Llanwarne, which was ten miles south of the city, by bike. He, his wife Ella and twin boys, Raymond and Christopher were staying on Hill Farm in the village. The farm belonged to Mr Spode, a cheery-faced shire horse breeder and distant relation of the famous china family. Hills Farm, however, was a culture shock for the Tomlinsons:

Bombed out: Barronia Metals manufactured this special fuel valve, which prevented fuel lines freezing on bombers flying at high altitude over enemy territory. When the West London factory was bombed, Barronia relocated to Hereford, along with engineer Albert West and his family. (*Herefordshire Lore/ In Our Age*)

> My mother gave up her well-appointed house in Twickenham for a farm where conditions were basic. There were no mains anything. Cooking was done on a twin paraffin burner which was always much hotter on one side than the other (I thought for a long time that it was normal for cakes to be black on one side). Sanitation consisted of a four-seater toilet down the garden.

Despite this, Ella Tomlinson learned to make cheese and butter, and to prepare rabbit, chicken and home-killed pig. 'I can remember a salted side of bacon hanging from hooks on the ceiling of the kitchen. When wriggly things started falling from it, the bad part was cut off and we ate the rest.' She learned to tolerate Jimmy Watkins, the farmhand with a passion for farm cider and a rich, agricultural language which he shared with the cattle as he milked them. Ella also learned to handle the recalcitrant farm pony. While her husband Reg rode his bicycle the 20 miles to and from work each day, Ella mastered the pony and trap, running the twins into town, and stabling the pony at the White Lion in Maylord Street, Hereford. When her shopping was done, the animal made its own way home with-out any guidance. 'The animal tolerated children, allowing them to ride on its back,' recalled Chris. 'But if a grown-up mounted the animal, the pony headed for the nearest low hanging tree branch. I cannot remember any adult, however good a horse person they were, who was not forced to return without the pony.'

By August of 1942, Reg, who had now acquired a car, was appointed chief designer of the company. He would soon begin working on fuel valves for a new secret weapon, the jet engine aircraft. He worked alongside production manager C.H. 'Tony' Williams. Tony and his family lived in the lodge at Bryngwyn Manor, Wormelow, and while he worked the customary long hours demanded by the war effort, he also indulged a passion for black and white photography, carrying his Leica with him wherever he went. When Barronia's managing director acquired the *Hereford Citizen and Bulletin* newspaper, Tony turned his hand to photojournalism. Long after the war Tony's daughter Dr Maureen Beauchamp discovered a tin trunk full of negatives and a collection of black and white films shot by her father at the factory. They formed the basis for a short film, *Hereford's Wartime Secrets*, in which men and women from the plant were seen posing nervously and smiling briefly at the camera. A succession of former workers came to see the film, including Evelyn Hill, Walter Williams, Dan Nash, Neville Dawe, Betty Webb, Peter Morris, Michael Wear, Margaret Palamountain, Doreen Oldman, Eric Mayers, Peter Yemm, Daphne Grey, Joyce Davis, Kitty Latham, Eve Lichfield, Joyce Mann, Gladys Jones, Mrs Short, Barbara Mitteen, Doug Parry, Donald Powell, Norman Owen, Carol Pritchard, Christine Harrison and Johnny Davey. When Carole Catley viewed the rushes she spotted her own father: 'It was eerie, stepping back in time.'

London to Llanwarne: Reg Tomlinson of Barronia, his wife Ella and their twin boys Raymond and Christopher left their comfortable Twickenham home and moved to Hill Farm, Llanwarne to live with shire horse breeder Mr Spode. 'With a four-seater toilet down the garden, no mains anything and a twin paraffin burner for cooking, the move to Llanwarne came as a shock to Ella,' recalled Christopher. 'But she learned to make cheese and butter, prepare rabbit, chicken and the home-killed pig, and manage the pony and trap when she needed to get to town. Father, meanwhile, rode his bike the ten miles to work at Barronia.' (*Christopher Tomlinson*)

In the autumn of 1945 Reg Tomlinson and another employee, Freddie Lichfield, who spoke perfect German, were selected as specialists to visit war-torn Germany to inspect the Nazi's progress with aircraft fuel valves. The men were issued with the uniforms of RAF Special Duties officers and had to conform to military discipline. 'They left on November 30 and I remember being allowed to stay up late on Christmas Eve waiting for his return,' recalled Chris. Their findings remained secret, but in the

Off to Germany: Reg (*left*) and Freddie Lichfield set off to inspect aircraft fuel valves in 1945. (*Herefordshire Lore/ In Our Age*)

post-war years Barronia Metals struggled to find new markets for their products. The company finally closed when Saunders Valves took over in January 1940, and the former buildings were eventually pulled down when a new inner city road was driven through the district.

13 On the Munitions

In terms of air raids Hereford suffered just one, pre-planned surgical air strike. The munitions factory, Royal Ordnance Factory Rotherwas, was hit in the early hours of 27 July 1942. Night-shift worker Lilian Summers ran outside to see what was going on. 'We were getting ready to go home,' recalled the then 20-year-old who had been putting cordite bundles into the shells and sewing cotton bags of cordite. 'Foolishly I looked up and I could clearly see the German swastika on the side of the plane.'

Home Guardsman Derek Adams had been camping in an orchard at Eign Hill, his loaded rifle beside him, when the German plane flew over. With no officer on hand to give orders, he stifled the urge to open fire and wondered, for the rest of his life, if he should have taken a potshot.

ROF Rotherwas was equipped with at least one defensive gun, but according to Albert Double of Standale Road, Hereford, an apprentice electrician at the factory on the day it was bombed, the gun could not be used:

> They [had] built a tower in front of the fireman's quarters with a Bren gun on top. Merchant navy men taught the Home Guard how to use it, and when the attack came two Home Guard [men] ran up the tower, but they could not get the ammunition because the major who had the key in his pocket was asleep in bed.

The Luftwaffe's target had been captured on film by a German spy plane two years earlier; the aerial images, seized by American military intelligence in Berlin at the war's end, depicting a peaceful scene below as chugging steam engines lined up to haul munitions out of the factory. The air strike, and the identity and numbers of those killed in the attack, were still subject to state secrecy 75 years later. The official silence led to people poring over the minute details of what happened; of how the enemy pilot appeared to wave at the workers below; of how a nearby orchard was draped with the clothes of the dead after the attack. Rumours continued to circulate that this had been a chance attack (although the Luftwaffe photographs suggest careful planning), and that the German pilot and his aircraft were brought down before they reached home.

Never dull (*left*): Lillian Summers started at the factory when she was 20, cleaning materials on 'Dirty Way', the section that was kept clear of explosive. She soon moved to 'Clean Way', where explosives were handled ('Clean' meant the workers were 'clean' of any materials, jewellery, cigarette lighters, matches, that could cause a spark). Lillian worked putting cordite bundles in the shells and chain-stitch sewing cotton bags of cordite. When the factory came under fire Lillian rushed outside: 'I ran out and looked up: I could clearly see the German swastika on the side of the plane.' She fled inside as the bombs fell. 'It was never dull down at Rotherwas.' (*Herefordshire Lore/ In Our Age*)

(*Right*) Bus pass: a worker's factory transport pass. ROF Rotherwas in Hereford had a huge impact on the local, mostly female, labour market with workers drawn from the Welsh Valleys, the Midlands and beyond to manufacture munitions. (*Pete Redding*)

One teenager central to the drama was the 16-year-old son of Ernest Hursey, the factory's chief inspector of police, Ken. Ernest and Bertha Hursey occupied Moorlands, the police house that stood outside the factory close to the south-western perimeter fence. 'We lived in a lovely old house, originally an old pub because it had a cider mill on the back of it, on the narrow lane to Dinedor Woods,' remembered Ken:

> The farmer lived under the hill and used to deliver the milk on his horse and cart. It was a beautiful summer that year. My eldest brother, 22-year-old Ernest, was in the Air Force training in Canada to become a pilot, and my second brother, 20-year-old Ronald, was home on leave from the army. Ernest's eldest brother's wife and her mum came down to stop with us for a week's holiday. So, being as

No defence: no anti-aircraft fire met the lone German bomber who attacked ROF Rotherwas in 1942. According to one witness, Albert Double, an apprentice electrician at the factory, the gun couldn't be deployed because the ammunition was under lock and key. Pictured in front of the gun (*front row, third from left*) is Thomas Williams: both he and his wife Florence worked at the factory. (*H. Pinnell*)

Empty shells: May Morgan (*second from right*) and colleagues work on empty shells. The photo may have been taken at one of the 'satellite' shell stores away from ROF Rotherwas. The main site was well known to the Germans, having been meticulously photographed by a Luftwaffe spy plane in 1940. (*Peggy Putnam*)

we had the visitors, my brother was in my bedroom, my older brother's wife and her mother were in the one bedroom and my mother and father were in the other bedroom. I was relegated to the cider mill at the back of the house.

It was very early, before six o'clock in the morning when the raid took place. The siren had gone off, but in those days nobody took any notice. I remember hearing the plane come over and I got out of bed and went to where I could look straight over the factory, and there was this plane swinging round and coming directly up the line of the sheds and almost directly in line with our house.

The bomb bay was open and then I saw the bombs come out. I think he dropped three bombs. The funny part about it is, although the first two exploded I can't remember any noise, any sound from them. You know, you just stand there transfixed and seeing this thing come and the place bursting and the flames going up?

And then I watched the third bomb come down. It came down inside the roof of one of the big sheds and then came bouncing out through the big doors where the trains used to go in. They used to run the trains in to pick up all the shells

Family tragedy: Ernest Hursey was chief inspector of the factory police, a job he loved. The war cost the lives of all but Ken, seen here standing beside his mother, Bertha. The bomb that hit their home, Moorlands on Watery Lane just outside the factory fence, killed Ernest and Bertha and their son Ronald. Ronald's wife Vera, 23, and his mother-in-law, Florence Carter, 47, were staying overnight. They also perished. Only Ken came out alive, being pulled from the ruins of the house. Two years later Ernest (*above right, in his flying gear*) crashed during a test flight on June 25, 1944, flying a Typhoon out of Hurn airfield. His plane was seen to spiral out of low cloud and crash a few miles north-west of Bournemouth. (*The Hursey family*)

and it bounced straight out of this big open door, bounced along the ground and cleared the perimeter fence and bounced straight into the front of our house. And everything from that moment was dead still.

I just turned round to run downstairs. I thought: "I'm going to tell my mum and dad that the bomb's hit the house." And, as I was halfway down the stairs, it exploded. It was probably on a short timed fuse so it wouldn't go off too soon. Had it exploded on impact it would have gone off in the factory, but it didn't; it just came and bounced over the ground into the front of the house and exploded.

After that all I remember, whether I was unconscious for a while, when I woke up everything was dead still and dead quiet. You couldn't hear a sound. It was so quiet.

I was buried under all the rubbish. I was still on the stairs, sideways on, and all the rubbish and brick and everything was on top of me. I tried to move, but I couldn't move. I shouted for my mum and dad as you naturally would do, but I couldn't get a sound out. I thought: "Where are they? They wouldn't leave me here." Then I heard somebody running down the lane. It was so quiet. Somebody says: "Is anybody about?" and I shouted: "Yes." I'm sure that was Mr Goodwin the farmer. And then eventually there were a lot of men down there, pushing and digging and shoving and they got a lot of the rubbish off me and I managed to move.

I knew they'd all been killed. It was obvious when the [rescuers] pulled me out. They just sat me still and I was looking round. There were curtains on the trees across the road. There was nothing, just a pile of rubble. It was only the thickness of the walls of the old building which stopped the blast from blowing me to kingdom come.

Bertha Hursey, 40, Ernest Hursey, 48, Florence Carter, 47, Vera Hursey, 23, and Ronald, 20, were all killed. In Ken's own words it was a tragic coincidence that his brother should be home on his first leave and his eldest brothers' family happened to be staying. The following March the now 17-year-old Ken joined the navy. He, alone of his family, survived the war. His second brother Ernest was killed in an air accident.

The bombing also killed an estimated 19 people inside a transit shed, including Ernest Henry Chesterman, 58, of Bridge House, Wye Bridge, Hereford; Daniel James Reginald Davies, 36, of Notts Cottage, Old Road, Bromyard; Frederick James Dyke, 47, of 3 Henry Street, Ross; William Garland, 45, of The Lodge, Vennwood, Bodenham; Edwin Gwilliam, 38, of Yew Tree Cottage, Christchurch, Coleford; David William Jenkins, 50, of 46 Belmont Avenue, Hereford (he died the following day); Beatrice Mary Saunders, 22, of Walkers House, Shelwick (she died four days later); James John Shine, 33, of 5 Paynters Terrace, Merthyr Tydfil; and Kathleen Blanche Wheeler, 31, of 72 Stonebow Road Hereford. Most of the dead were buried in an unmarked grave at Bullinghope Church. Edwin Gwilliam's daughter, Mrs T.J. Brown, wrote later: 'My father had been on night work, so he would have been getting ready to catch the bus home. For many years I couldn't understand why he seemed to be the only one killed. Everything was kept secret because of the war.'

Shadow units: Jim Henderson's garage at Whitney-on-Wye (*opposite, top*) was kitted-out with machine tools, under the U.S. Lend-Lease scheme, to make vital parts for allied aircraft. The 30-strong workforce of country women worked two shifts on a twelve-hour day, six days a week. One of the first employees was Hazel Evans (*above, centre with friends*) from Whitney. In the early 1940s, Hazel met Londoner Bob Rayner who, being fluent in French and German, had been recruited to the Intelligence Corps attached to the 49th Division and was stationed at Whitney Court. They married at Whitney Church in 1943 (*left*), shortly before Bob left for the 1944 D-Day landings at Juno Beach. He was an interpreter during the German surrender, and was later posted to Germany to interrogate former Nazis. 'It wasn't easy for Bob and Hazel to adjust to peace time,' remembers daughter Jenny Hill. (*Tom Henderson and Jenny Hill*)

The Royal Ordnance Factory had been shrouded in secrecy from its inception. Brought into operation during the First World War the factory, by May 1944, employed 2,700 people, 2,000 of them women. The payroll for so many employees required the services of over 50 staff including one young mum, Marie Hill. 'On the payroll we would work out how many notes and half-crowns [the pay] came to. Then it would go into the cash office and the cash office would put up the money.' They would count out the money, put it in the pay packets and then hand it out on pay day, working in pairs to reduce the risk of errors. Mistakes did happen. 'One time we were short by half-a-crown. We went up and down this payroll and the pay packets and could not find it. In the end the supervisor took our names down and put it in the book [that] we'd pinched half-a-crown.'

ROF Rotherwas was not the only munitions works in the county. Alf Evans recalled several smaller 'shadow' units in the countryside:

> We used to have one or two small shadow factories [where] they used to make little components. In a village somebody perhaps had a big garage and it was turned into making some component for aircraft. There was one out on the Hay road, just beyond Whitney Bridge. Ledbury had one or two places; they also had the searchlights unit there.

Kit Hodges (then Kit Gower) worked in one such satellite factory at Withington, preparing nuts and bolts for military aircraft. She had been working as a domestic servant – 'Seven and six pence-a-week, and I can't tell you how many hours I had to work' – when she switched to the war work. 'They put me on dipping all these nuts and bolts in this mucky stuff. I used to get filthy, so I said to the boss: "Can I have a different job?" He said: "If you don't like it you can go up the road." I thought: "Oh well!"' (Kit would shortly leave and join the ATS – *see 'Wrens and the ATS', page 117*).

Any industrial operation is prone to accidents and ROF Rotherwas was no exception. On 21 September 1941 a milling machine overheated, its contents exploding and killing George MacLaren, Francis Hicks and Henry Bigglestone. D.C. Booton was working on an automatic telephone exchange at Rotherwas when the explosion shook the equipment. 'I dashed outside to see a large pall of smoke rising above one of the sheds,' he recalled.

Years later a young woman from the Forest of Dean, Clohilda Dickinson, also recalled the explosion. One of a family of ten then living at Christchurch, Coleford, Clohilda had been working at Lyons Bakery in London during the Blitz. With two brothers at war – Donald with General Montgomery's Eighth Army and another fleeing Singapore as the Japanese occupied the city – Clohilda volunteered for munitions work.

I presented myself at Rotherwas and was given a strict medical examination and pronounced fit and ready to start work. Working with high explosives, we worked alternate shifts of days and afternoon and nights. My day shift would start as I boarded the bus at 5 a.m. for the 35-mile ride to the factory. As we entered the gates, special police carried out random searches – woe betide anyone entering with a match on their person.

In the changing rooms we donned a coat, overalls with our identification number sprawled across our backs, little pillbox hats made of the same non-flammable material and special shoes without nails.

Clohilda Dickinson: the munition worker from the Forest of Dean narrowly escaped injury in two separate incidents at ROF Rotherwas. (*Sandra Watson*)

Clohilda was sent to fill shells with explosives at Unit 2 on the South Side, the most dangerous section of the factory. The toxic chemicals turned women's skin and hair yellow, despite free baths and milk to counter its effects. The startling discolouration earned the women their nickname: the Canaries.

'Even wearing masks it was impossible to avoid absorbing the deadly TNT and it began to take its toll,' recalled Clohilda. One day when she felt too ill to work she was allowed out. 'Taking a book I sat on a grassy slope where I could breathe the fresh air.'

Moments later the explosion ripped through the mill where she had been working, killing three of her fellow male workers.

Those whose work brought them into direct contact with the explosives took it in turns to have a weekly bath. Many women suffered from poisoning at ROF Rotherwas. Mrs Pitman from Lydney suffered TNT poisoning while working with two others in a cubicle filling 25-pound bombs – 'I was dispatched for a few months under Dinmore Hill going through [empty munition] cases' – while Mrs Winders from Worcester became 'very ill and jaundiced' from the toxic effects of painting shells yellow.

Clohilda took up the story again:

> The bathrooms were a great distance from the factory proper, and we were allowed the time to have our bath during working hours. This night the leading hand came to me and told me to take the last bath of the shift. I calculated that by the time I had finished my bath it would be the end of our shift and I would not have to go back to the unit where I worked.

She was feeling 'fresh and clean after washing away the horrible powder' when the German bomber appeared, and the attack that would kill so many workers began.

The bombing did not seriously damage operations at the factory. Vera Mary Oakley was back 'filling the empty bomb shells with TNT' the following day. She had narrowly escaped injury during the attack:

> I arrived early for my 6.00 a.m. shift on the South Side [the factory was divided into North and South sections by the Straight Mile Road that divided the site], but went into the canteen for a cup of tea. A few minutes later I would have been there, where the bombs fell, clocking my card to start work.

Badly shaken, Vera walked the five miles home to the family farm at Allensmore.

However, production *was* severely disrupted by an explosion in 1944. Alfred Parry and his wife Violet, both munitions workers at Rotherwas in the First World War, were now living with their munitions worker daughter Josephine at 17 Venns Close Alms House. Alfred broke the news of this explosion in a letter dated 1 June to his second daughter Doll living in London:

Dear Doll,

Just a line to let you know we are alright, and hoping to find you all in a better state of health. I expect you heard on the wireless of the excitement and in many ways a catastrophe for Hereford which occurred on Tuesday evening about 7.30. We had finished tea and Jose had gone up to lay on the bed for half an hour and I was sat at the little table under the window in the front room with the window open, as it was very hot as we had thunderstorms earlier

when all of a sudden a tremendous explosion occurred which fairly rocked the town, and the blast of air rushed through the window and fairly dazed me for seconds and the bedroom doors swung back with a thud and Jose started bellowing out.

Loads of men and trailer pumps were going over the Wye Bridge down to the factory. After the first explosion the fire fighting service connected with the factory had begun to function when the second lot of bombs began to explode which put the men and their appliances Hors De Combat and fires started in all directions. They say the Yanks did splendid service there especially the coloured chaps, they rushed in irrespective of danger and did good work, there was dozens of jeeps and USA red cross van and stretchers and USA mobile canteen in service, so there

US aid: Alfred Parry wrote to his daughter, Doll, after a series of accidental explosions at the factory in 1944: 'They say the Yanks did splendid service there, especially the coloured chaps, they rushed in irrespective of danger.' (*Brian Millington*)

is no work for Jose this week, nor the other girls and it don't look very healthy about ever starting again there. They are paying the three shifts their last weeks wages on Friday afternoon.

Cheerio and all the best, Dad XXXXX

Jose was laid off shortly after (she died of TB the following year) because the Hereford Incident, as it became known, had caused serious damage. The 'incident' had started on 30 May with a fire in a South Section shed followed by an explosion. Eight hundred workers were evacuated before a second explosion, which sent sheets of flame 2,000 feet into the air, resounded across the countryside, shattering windows nearby. Five-year-old Chris Tomlinson heard the explosion at Llanwarne almost ten miles away. Chorister Griff Loydd was emerging from choir practice at Holy Trinity Church in Whitecross Road, Hereford. 'There came a devil of a bang and a huge cloud of black smoke.' His father John Richard Jones worked on the munitions and Griff ran home to Kings Acre Road to check on 'my dear Dad.' To his relief he found his father still preparing for work.

The following year the *London Gazette* reported that there had been three consecutive explosions following the fire, which had started in a bomb. Despite the frantic efforts of a group of men who fought the fire for 20 minutes, the bomb detonated, demolishing the explosives filling house. 'Sixteen men ignored the danger to save their work mates,' reported the *Gazette*, listing the George Medal bravery awards given to Nick St Vincent de Lisle Carey, Frederick Tyler, Frederick Lewis, James Little and fireman Harold Davies. Five firemen (W. 'Jack' Davies from Allensmore, Alfred 'Joe' Chamberlain, J. Jenkins, Albert Haynes and A. Morris), two overlookers (T. Boucher and E. Bromley) and two electricians (C. Bennett and J. Breen) received the British Empire Medal. The factory superintendent, R.E.D. Owens and the chief technical assistant W.L. Fitzmaurice, who later defused 1,500 pounds of explosives, respectively received an OBE and an MBE.

Nick St Vincent de Lisle Carey and his family had only recently escaped the German occupation of Guernsey, leaving his sister Marguerite behind. She overheard, on an illegal wireless set, news of an explosion at an ammunition factory 'somewhere in the West Country' and feared the worst.

Albert Haynes' son-in-law Terry Harris recalled how Bert, whose older son Bryan had already been killed by a truck at Rotherwas in 1944, 'always maintained he was making the tea' at the time. 'In fact he was perched on top of the 2,000 pound bomb playing a hose over it to keep it cool.' Joe Chamberlain's daughter-in-law Margaret believed the firemen escaped serious injuries when the bomb exploded because the blast went over their heads.

Two men died: 41-year-old Fred Raper of 31 Ants Nest, Church Street, Ledbury and 50-year-old special constable William Constantine Walton of the Residence, Kenchester. William's nephew Trevor Watkins from Credenhill remembered the blast:

> I was with friends close to Mill Farm, Credenhill and the farm windows were blown open by a blast: we thought the explosion was on the RAF station. Later the terrible news of William's death was brought to my father. There was further anxiety as my mother waited for news of her sister, Irene Winney, who had been working on the same shift. Eventually we learned she was safe.

Years later Trevor recalled William Walton's funeral cortège passing The Residence at Kenchester on its way to Kenchester Church.

Aside from accidents, life at ROF Rotherwas involved long hours and hard, mostly dull work. It had its compensations, however. One woman, who described the munitions as 'all work and bed', was glad of the 4d extra an hour paid for working with explosives on the South Side, and spoke of the shared excitement when her workmates filled their first 1,000 pound bomb.

Vera Oakley recalled her 21st birthday on the factory floor:

> I was friendly with the foreman and some lunch times he would put in a request for the song, *Oh You Beautiful Doll*, on the factory radio [the factory ran its own radio

station]. On my birthday he picked me up and carried me through the sheds singing *Twenty-one Today*. We made our own fun, often singing songs from 4.00 a.m. onwards to keep awake. The downside was working with TNT which often turned your hands and hair yellow. You weren't allowed to wear jewellery due to the risk of sparks and an explosion, and the Danger Man, as we called him, would patrol the factory to make sure everyone complied. But the foreman would step in and place any jewellery we had under his hat till Danger Man had gone.

Another munitions worker, Gladys, left the factory in 1944, her skin still discoloured from contact with the explosives, to marry farmer Bill Christopher. 'I married on April 17. My skin was still yellow, but it soon faded. And with the money I saved at the factory I was able to buy three cows.'

Tel. No. :   Gerrard 6933.
              Extn. 1022 & 888

MINISTRY OF SUPPLY

SHELL MEX HOUSE,
STRAND,
LONDON, W.C.2.

Our Reference :

Your Reference :

9th January, 1945.

Dear Mr. Barrington,

      It has been brought to my attention by the Superintendent, R.O.F. Hereford, that, on the occasion of the explosion and fire at that Factory, you hurried from your home with all speed and assisted in every way possible to relieve the sufferings of the casualties both in the Surgery and by bringing them from the scene of the fire.

      As Director-General of the Filling Factories, I should like to take this opportunity of congratulating you on your courageous behaviour, which, however, comes as no surprise to me, as I am aware that you acted in just as loyal and humane a manner on the occasion some two years ago when your colleagues at the Factory were in distress.

      I should like to thank you for the great help you rendered.

With kind regards,

Yours sincerely,

C.S. Robinson

DIRECTOR-GENERAL: FILLING FACTORIES.

Courageous behaviour: A letter sent to senior St John Ambulance man Len Barrington for his bravery following the explosion of May 1944. (*Elaine and Allan Brewer*)

14 The War Above

Patriotism played a significant role in the decision of women like Gladys Christopher to join ROF Rotherwas. Iris Watkins from Dilwyn served overseas with the ATS (*see 'Wrens and the ATS', page 117*). She echoed the view of many munition workers: 'We all had to go and do our job. It seems very unreal now, but people are patriotic aren't they? They put their country first.' Men and women, particularly those involved in the munitions, were keenly aware that they were manufacturing weapons that would kill soldiers and civilians alike: 'What a terrible thing it is to think we men [were] working our lives out to blow other people to pieces,' as railway man Sidney Keates put it. He staffed the trains shuttling munitions between ROF Rotherwas and Moreton-on-Lugg.

The biggest threat to civilians, both home and abroad, came from the air, and many Hereford people worked in military aviation. Charles Price of Pilley Road had been apprenticed to Ravenhills in Commercial Street at the age of 11, but went on to build Blenheim bombers for Bristol Aircraft until 1937, when he moved to 25th Maintenance Unit at Kidderminster working on Merlin engines. 'I was two years on balancing the propellers; they had to be spot on.'

Women, too, worked in aviation. Betty Macklin joined the Women's Auxiliary Air Force (WAAF) at the age of 19 and trained in Gloucester, Morecambe ('doing physical

Counting them back: Joan Lloyd was an RAF telephonist based at Bomber Command RAF Binbrook, Lincolnshire. 'Sometimes we did night duty and you could count planes going out; we knew how many hadn't made it when we counted them coming back.' Joan would later teach demobbed airmen her switchboard skills at RAF Credenhill. (*Joan Lloyd*)

training on the sea front with everyone looking!') and Kirkham before serving in Llandeilo with the 53rd Officer Training Corps. A tragic coincidence brought her home to Herefordshire: 'I lost two brothers, one at sea and one in the Air Force within three months.' She returned to be closer to her distraught mother ('she was paid ten shillings a week to have me there') and to work at RAF Madley, where she was responsible for ordering parts for the aircraft, single-winged Proctors and twin-winged de Havilland Dominies. She soon took to the air herself. 'They [RAF Madley staff] thought, because I was ordering parts, I'd better go up in one.' Issued with a parachute she flew over Hereford to Malvern and back.

Enemy aircraft regularly passed over Herefordshire, although the city was said to have its own guardian angel protecting it from attack. According to Father Brendan Minney, a monk at Belmont Abbey, the figure of Christ erected over St Xavier's Church in Broad Street gave the city its protection. Hereford, he promised, would never be bombed so long as the statue remained on top of the church. The figure had been carved by Charles Gertner who served with allied forces in the First World War (Gertner, ironically, had fallen foul of Herefordshire Council when he was initially appointed to the Art School staff towards the end of the war. Alderman James Corner complained that he 'sounded' German. Gertner came from Wales). Gertner's statue remained looking down on Broad Street until the 1950s when, after a spell neglected in a builder's yard, it disappeared.

Hereford city did escape the bombings, although Frances Coleman recalled seeing a German flare fall in Blueschool Street as she travelled to Painter Brothers on board a National Auxiliary Fire Service truck from the fire station. Other parts of the county, including Rotherwas, were less fortunate. Alf Evans, a deputy head warden in Lower Bullingham was one of the first on the scene of the Rotherwas bombing described earlier by Ken Hursey. 'I heard the two bombs drop at seven in the morning. It was only over the road so I got on my bike and went down. I had to dive in the ditch because the plane came right over Holme Lacy Road, about 500 foot up.' Alf cycled up Watery Lane:

> The first bomb had landed near the perimeter of the factory killing a number of employees. The second bomb had dropped on the house in Watery Lane and demolished it. There had been five houses there; now there were only four. It was eerie. There was just the sounds of dripping water from a broken tap, a terrific smell – sometimes I smell that same smell in the river weed and it brings the memory back – and bodies steaming.

Meanwhile the number of random aerial bombings in the county was mounting and people volunteered to join others on night time 'fire-watching' duties. One county librarian recalled how they shared their watch with county council staff:

> Having been taught to operate stirrup pumps, and issued with camp beds and itchy blankets, we slept in the Education Department. One of our crew was the

pathologist, a good story-teller, but neither bombs nor eerie tales frightened us as much as the sound of mice scrabbling in waste paper baskets near our ears.

Many bombs were dropped by the enemy jettisoning their load due to mechanical problems. Philip Hughes (*Wings Over the Wye*) described bombs falling at Kilforge House, Ballingham; Hellens at Much Marcle; the White House, Turnastone; the Chase at Ross; and Kingstone, Hope under Dinmore, Llanigon, Aston Crews, Staunton and Cradley. Bruce Leonard, meanwhile, recalled another at Ocle Pychard. Bruce had been evacuated to the village from London when the Blitz began. 'I wasn't very old, five or six, and I remember having a label tied to my coat lapel with my name and address on when I arrived at Barrs Court Station.' He was put on board a Midland Red bus to Ocle Pychard, and remained there through the war, living with the Adams family at Waterloo Cottage on Tom Pearson's farm. 'It was idyllic and I was in heaven. Then one night we were woken up by very loud bangs – I knew straight away what they were, but was too frightened to say anything. I thought Hitler had followed me from London.' The next day they investigated the bomb crater left in the farm orchard and learned that 'poor Mr Jancy's calves and chickens had been blown up into a tree'.

Shadowed by Hitler: Bruce Leonard was evacuated from London to Ocle Pychard as a boy. When bombs began falling near the village his worst fears were realised: 'I thought Hitler had followed me from London.' (*Bruce Leonard*)

Aerial accidents were also becoming more common. Ray Bird was working at the Central Garage, Kington when he witnessed a collision between two aircraft. He had just turned 14 and was working at Alf Edwards' garage opposite the Burton Hotel when the two aircraft flew into each other above the woods. The collision destroyed the wing on one plane and the tail on the second. All four crew on board the planes were killed.

Hereford teacher Bill Morris, then a flying officer navigator with Bomber Command, was lying in the grass on a Midlands airfield waiting for his turn on board a Wellington bomber in June 1944. The aeroplane, which had taken off after a major overhaul, had several air instructors on board who were carrying out a thorough air test. 'The Wellington reached about 1,000 feet. It banked steeply and, with horror, we saw its starboard wing fall off. The plane crashed about a mile away killing all the crew.'

Ada Eacock was deeply traumatised when she witnessed the crash of a British bomber in southern England:

> Bernard my husband, then a corporal in the Royal Tank Corps, and I went on a picnic down by the docks and we heard this drove of planes going out. Then my husband said to me: "There's one in trouble." This big bomber was twirling around and around and then boof! It exploded. And of course everyone in it was killed.

Ada was expecting their second child. 'The crash upset me so much that I was hysterical. I went to bed, but woke up screaming.' Bernard, who was due to rejoin his regiment the next day, refused to leave her side. He was arrested for being absent without leave and given three days in prison. Back in his regiment later, Bernard fought at the Battle of El Alamein. When he went missing, Ada was told he was 'presumed dead'. Eventually Bernard turned up, wounded but alive, in a Cairo hospital.

Ada would witness another air incident when she and Bernard were living with a local couple, Mr and Mrs Morgan, near Aldershot. A German aircraft dropped a bomb nearby ('Mr Morgan was in the toilet and the blast blew him off the seat!') and then strafed neighbouring houses: 'The pilot came down and peppered all the sheets, hanging on the washing lines, with a machine gun.'

Ron Hodges, then a 13-year-old evacuee living in Chepstow, also witnessed an enemy attack, this time on the Army Technical School for Boys at Beachey Camp. A lone German, 'a Dornier, I think,' bombed and strafed the school, killing one boy and badly wounding a soldier. Ron had been out fishing: 'The pilot was following the Wye down (a good navigation aid I suppose). He was so close I could see the crosses on the plane.' Ron had only recently escaped the London blitz. 'I saw the beginning of it before I was sent to Chepstow. Just after I left, my sister Catherine told me how some incendiaries had landed on the linoleum factory next to West Ham football ground.' Inflammable rolls of linoleum had risen into the air, uncurling as they burned and floating above the houses like magic carpets. 'Oh you missed a sight, Ron,' she told her brother.

It was a sight also missed by the London-based author of the *Chronicles of Narnia*, C.S. 'Jack' Lewis. Then on a speaking tour for his popular Christian Life Campaign, he was staying with the Bishop in Hereford and sharing his thoughts on children's literature with Joy Parsons, the Bishop's daughter-in-law. 'He asked for some children's books as bedside reading, as respite from the London Blitz and I introduced him to *Baba The Elephant*' (his courteous note of thanks is lodged with the Bodleian Library).

Herefordshire's churches escaped any bomb damage. Its parishioners, however, were ready to help others. When the parish church of Chilvers Coton near Coventry was destroyed by bombs in 1941, worshippers at St James Church in Hereford heard of their plight (the respective ministers of St James and Chilvers Coton had been at theological college together). St James raised £500 (about £20,000 today) towards the rebuilding of the church.

The Luftwaffe's Hans Seidemann who, ironically, had flown over the Herefordshire countryside seven years before the war, directed many of the aerial attacks against Britain. He had been a guest of wealthy air ace Randolph Trafford from Michaelchurch Escley. Trafford had his own private airfield, and in 1934 invited several German fliers to visit. A young lad from Garway, Les Rowlands, had been on a visit to Mr Howard, the tailor at Michaelchurch, to have his school suit made up. He and the tailor set off to watch Trafford and his guests demonstrate their aerial skills:

> We joined a small group of spectators and were given a spectacular display of stunts, especially the falling leaf [a stall and spin manoeuvre]. One of the planes had swastikas on its wings and we little thought that those planes would be back in about ten years' time to rain down bullets on us.

Seidemann had led the Luftwaffe attack against the Republicans during the Spanish Civil War, which had brought Josefina Carmen and her Basque refugees to Hereford. Another pilot flying the swastika over Michaelchurch Escley that day was Alexander

Growing older by the week: Brian Davies described flying long distance bombers, after being a fighter pilot, as like becoming a bus driver. He and his crew survived a long tour of duty and gave short shrift to the publican who grumbled about the crew drinking his beer. Brian, 23 (*back row, second from right*): 'It was a tradition that, when you finished your tour, you were photographed with your crew and ground crew; a tour being, theoretically, 30 bombing trips. I was a young man growing older by the week.' (*Brian Davies*)

von Winterfeldt, credited with bringing down many allied pilots during the Battle of Britain. Winterfeldt was killed in a flying accident. Trafford, who had joined the Royal Navy Volunteer Reserve, died when his Fairey Fulmar crashed on Dartmoor in January 1943 (he was buried at Michaelchurch). Seidemann, who escaped the Nuremberg trials of Nazi war criminals, died in the 1960s.

Like Trafford, many Herefordshire men, and several women, joined the air services. Brian Davies had trained as a fighter pilot, but after a spell at RAF Shobdon, was dispatched to RAF Abingdon to form part of a bomber crew. 'This was a very do-it-yourself job: pilots, navigators, bomb aimers, wireless operators and rear gunners were all put into a room and told 'in an hour's time you are to come out as crews'. Brian had his reservations about piloting a bomber – 'You'd spent a long time flying single-engine aircraft and suddenly they want you to become a bus driver' – but as an experienced pilot with 700 flying hours to his name he was a catch for any crew. Eventually, a ginger-haired Australian rear gunner singled him out and, having discovered Davies' commendable flying record, rounded up a navigator, bomb aimer and wireless operator, all Australians.

The new crew had their first bonding experience not in the air, but over a pint at a local pub:

> We walked in and shouted for six pints of bitter. The landlord grumbled: "Don't know why you're coming up here drinking my beer, [when] you've got plenty up the camp." I knew we were going to be a good crew because the Aussie navigator, only a little fellow with a great lock of blond hair, looked at me. And everybody else looked at each other (…) and then we picked up our pints, drank half and then turned them upside down on the bar and walked out. Not a word was spoken.

Brian survived his tour of duty. He was lucky. Jim Thomas recalled the fate of a friend who joined another bomber crew:

> You had to be a very, very educated bloke to get your head blown off in the Air Force. One school friend who achieved air-crew status was Cyril Cotterell, and I remember how very proud he was that a chap who had nothing more than an elementary education achieved navigator status in the RAF.

Cyril and his sister lived in a cottage by the Canny Brook near Barrs Court railway station. 'The last conversation I had with Cyril was outside the Commercial in Commercial Road. We were both on home leave at the time. He said: "Well I've passed out now and I am going to a Pathfinders Squadron."' The Pathfinder Force was used to mark targets by dropping flares for the bombers that followed.

'Cyril said: "I'm very proud, of course, but I probably won't come back." I said: "Don't talk so damn stupid." But I knew, in our own squadron, only about 4% of chaps achieved a tour of about 20 or 30 operations. Of course, Cyril didn't.'

Douglas Hughes also recalled losing his best friend, John Tillam whose father, Jack, ran the butcher's shop opposite the Lamb Hotel in St Owen Street. 'John was shot down over Holland in 1944.'

Some British pilots found it hard to put their flying days behind them when back on terra firma. One former Spitfire test pilot from Gloucester, Michael Daunt, was given time off to recover from stress and sent to recuperate at Castle Frome, helping with the hop picking. His jobs included pumping water from a brook into a tank pulled by the tractor and then hauling it back to the buildings. The tractor had never before been driven so fast, and eventually, despite warnings, Michael and his machine ended up in the brook. Michael escaped unhurt and returned to flying, often passing low or performing loop-the-loops over the farmhouse and fields.

Women took to the air too. Marjorie Rosser had left school at the age of 15 and, having learned Pitman shorthand and typing, started work in the offices of Dunlop Rubber near her hometown of Liverpool. In 1942 she was conscripted into the WAAFs. 'I became a flight engineer at RAF Rednal, an officers' training unit in Shropshire. We'd fill the kites up with petrol in the morning and empty the tanks at night.' There were distinct, if dangerous, advantages to working alongside the boys in blue. 'We had two-seater training Spitfires at Rednal and sometimes we'd be taken up for a ride: we flew in our ordinary battledress – no special training or anything.'

Flying Spitfires: Marjorie Rosser (*above and overleaf*) was conscripted into the Women's Auxiliary Air Force, the WAAFs in 1942. As a flight engineer at RAF Rednal, she prepared – and sometimes flew in – the training officers' two-seater Spitfires. One morning she was alarmed to find a stowaway German POW hiding in a plane. Later, sharing a cup of cocoa with him, she had to concede: 'he was the most gorgeous young man I ever saw in my life.' (*Marjorie Rosser*)

Marjorie, who would eventually move to Hereford, had a shock when she checked her planes one morning. 'There was a German prisoner of war, curled up asleep inside the cockpit. I screamed and everyone came running.' The POW took a shine to Marjorie:

> Later, before he was returned to his POW camp, we all had cocoa, but he wouldn't drink his until I had been brought over to stand by his side (he was only a boy, but I have to say he was the most gorgeous young man I ever saw in my life).

Back in Herefordshire, RAF Madley, a busy training station with three grass runways mainly designed to serve as a school for wireless operators, had been operational since August 1941. The building of the airfield had a significant impact on the district. One villager recalled how the construction workers were billeted on the locals. 'You had to take workmen in if you had room. We had two from Wales staying with us: they were very nice.' According to Philip Hughes in *Wings Over the Wye* it was home to No. 4 Signals School and the No. 8 Anti-Aircraft Co-operation Unit. They were relocated here while the old Pembridge Landing Ground was upgraded, and reopened in May 1942 as Shobdon Airfield.

Betty Macklin had mixed feelings about the new residents at RAF Madley:

> There were lots of airmen at RAF Madley, including two Americans who kept a Tiger Moth [biplane] on the airfield. They used to come and sit by our fire and they gave me their white cat when they left. They didn't say it was a she-cat: there were white kittens all over the place when they'd gone!

One secret visitor to RAF Madley was the German, Rudolf Hess. Hess, third in command of Adolf Hitler's wartime cabinet had flown to Scotland in 1941 claiming to be on a peace mission to Britain. Angela Francis, working in a jam factory at Madley, spotted Hess under guard, having a cigarette beside a plane parked on the airfield. Hess may have been on his way to Maindiff Court Military Hospital at Abergavenny where he was held for three years.

Another unexpected visitor to RAF Madley was a Lancaster bomber. Sixteen-year-old Valerie Tilby was working on a neighbouring farm at the time:

> My family, Dad and Mum – Ted and Winnie – and my sister Beryl had moved out of London to Cardiff where Dad, who had already served in the First World War, was a recruiting officer. When the bombing intensified we moved to Cherry Orchard Cottage in Blakemere with Dad working at RAF Madley and my sister in the Land Army.
>
> Dad's brother, Edward 'Ted' Tilby, was serving with the RAF as a bomb aimer on Lancasters. One day in 1944 Dad's Austin 7 arrived at our house with Ted and the rest of the crew of a Lancaster bomber, all except the pilot, crammed in the car. They had landed at RAF Madley and they stopped with us for tea. They were very young and gung ho and they went back to Madley laughing about how people said they'd never clear the hedges on take-off.
>
> Minutes later the 'plane flew over, dipping its wings as it headed home!

Ted and the crew did not make it through the war. According to Valerie the aircraft was brought down after an attack on the German destroyer *Tirpitz*. Although the Lancaster made a sea 'landing' off the Norwegian coast, the crew were killed by machine gun fire as they tried to board a rescue boat.

Marjorie Rosser: conscripted into the WAAFs (Women's Auxiliary Air Force) in 1942. (*Marjorie Rosser*)

Tupsley air crash: several children witnessed the fatal air accident involving 24-year-old Pilot Officer Bill Binnie and his trainee radio operator Corporal Nutter in January 1944. Bill Binnie's Proctor crashed in Tupsley after losing its port wing, killing both airmen, according to Bill's son Steve. Steve Binnie never met his father: 'I was born a few weeks later and my mother never really talked about my father's death.' (*Steve Binnie*)

Meanwhile, the arrival of so many young men in RAF uniform was welcomed by many, not least some of the women now studying to become teachers at the Hereford Training College. They were asked to provide 'morale boosting social sessions for the troops', which involved Saturday evenings spent dancing, playing cards, table tennis and darts – not only with the airmen at Madley and Credenhill, but also with the English and American soldiers stationed across the county. Jean Muldowney remembered, as a girl peeping through a crack in the door of the Key Hostel, a dance hall next to the Odeon Theatre. 'I used to peer in and watch American soldiers dancing the jitterbug. It was an amazing sight! I wished that I was older and able to join in.'

One Land Army girl, who went on to marry a Blakemere farmer, initially stayed at a Land Army hostel at Blakemere House. She remembered visits from the airmen at Madley, and joining them on the dance floor at village hall hops.

Romances were inevitable and, just as inevitably, some ended in tragedy. Thomas Pitt had been training as a radio operator at RAF Madley when he became engaged to local girl, Joan Hiles. They would never marry. Pitt died when the Halifax bomber in which he was radio operator and rear gunner crashed in Nottingham returning from a bombing raid over Germany.

With three training stations in Herefordshire (Madley, Credenhill and Shobdon) local air accidents were becoming commonplace. On Sunday 30 January 1944, school-girl Margaret Bentley-Leek looked up when an airplane flew overhead. Her idle curiosity turned to horror when she saw a wing fall away from the aircraft. She ran home to tell her parents, but no-one took her seriously until word reached the family that a Percival Proctor from RAF Madley had crashed nearby. John Slatford had been parading with the Home Guard outside the Rose and Crown:

> We heard the bang and saw the plane go down. My platoon ran the quarter of a mile through the old brick field – the 'Brickie' as we called it – and came on the crash site in the middle of my father's allotment in the garden of The Knoll.

The plane had been flown by 24-year-old Flying Officer Bill Binnie. Years later the pilot's son Steve learned more about the aircraft's fate after hearing these eyewitness accounts. Steve Binnie had never met his father: 'I was born a few weeks after he was killed and my mother never really talked about his death.' The Proctor had been on a routine flight with Bill Binnie and a 20-year-old trainee operator, Corporal Nutter. Bill was an accomplished pilot. He had joined the RAF in 1937 and recently returned from the Empire Flying Training School in Canada. Initially a rigger on early Tiger Moths, he had flown Spitfires on aerial reconnaissance before being sent to Madley to shuttle around the young radio operator trainees. The Proctor had crashed after losing its port wing.

Another crash on 22 October the following year shook the inhabitants of Preston Wynne. The aircraft, a Short Stirling bomber, flight EF 352, with a crew of nine appeared to have gone into a vertical dive and exploded on impact at Rosemaund Farm. The crew were all killed. Ron Miles, then a lad of 15, had cycled to the crash site. He remembered the event for the rest of his life, and in 1997 presented the surviving widow of the then 21-year-old wireless operator and air gunner, Jack McMillan, with a home-made model of the aircraft. The cause of the crash was never revealed.

The high ground of west Herefordshire, out towards the Brecon Beacons, brought down many wartime aircraft. Still based at RAF Madley, Betty Macklin recalled how pilots would engage in mock dog fights over the Black Mountains. She was horrified when one aircraft came down killing the pilot. 'I remember his kit coming back into Madley. I picked up this glove and this airman said: "That's got a hand in it." He was joking.'

Black Mountains crash: Ascend Charlie, Flight 42-5903 was returning from Bordeaux on 16 September 1943 to its base, RAF Framlingham in Suffolk, when, due to bad weather and the loss of one engine struck by anti-aircraft fire, it hit the summit of Pen Gwyllt Meirch, 1,800 feet up on the Black Mountains. All ten crew were killed. The plane was piloted by 22-year-old Herbert Turner (*front row, second from left*) and the average age of the crew was just 22. Wilbur Hoffman (*back row, third from left*) was in this picture, but escaped the disaster having stepped down from that night's flight. (*Herefordshire Lore/ In Our Age*)

Jack Wakefield from Lincolnshire met his wife-to-be in 1942 'in the glamorous sur-rounds of a NAAFI dance at RAF Credenhill'. On 2 August, however, Jack was close to St Mary's hospital (then Burghill Asylum) when an American B-24 Liberator came down:

> I was only a field or so away when the badly shot-up Liberator crashed in the grounds. With bullets and cannon shells flying everywhere and the aircraft burning fiercely, there was little we could do to help, although most of the crew would have been killed in combat or on impact [in fact, eight crew died and two survived].

One of the strangest crashes involved another American Liberator which crashed on Christmas day, 1944 above Vowchurch Common with no one on board: the crew had bailed out over Germany and France.

Len Roberts investigated the circumstances of over 30 crashes in his booklet for the Royal Air Force Association (*Air Crash Sites and the Stories Behind Them*, revised 2010),

RAF Madley: Air crew Dennis Beavan (*left*) with 'Taffy' Bounds began training as wireless operators at Madley around 1944, flying in de Havilland Dominies ('eight of us at a time') before graduating to two-seater Proctors such as the one that crashed on Tupsley. Until then, Dennis had worked as one of the 'Stonebow messenger boys', trained by Superintendent Weaver to tour the city giving out information if Hereford came under attack. (*Dennis Beavan*)

listing seven in the Black Mountains. They included the Flying Fortress 42-5903 'Ascend Charlie' in which all ten crew died (struck by anti-aircraft fire over La Rochelle, France on 16 September 1943, it had been flown home by 22-year-old Herbert Turner); and an Anson that hit the ground just to the north of Capel-y-ffin on 21 September 1942 without loss of life. This crew was lucky. The pilot of another Anson (N9879), Flight Lieutenant R.M. Nobiston, on a training flight from the same observers' navigation school at Staverton on 2 March 1940, was killed, while his three crew escaped serious injury. The plane crashed southeast of the trig point on Hay Bluff.

Another pilot lost his life when his U.S. Lightning aircraft (42-67859) from 402 Fighter Squadron USA 8th Army Air Force, Andover, struck the western slopes of the Olchon Valley in low cloud on 12 April 1944. And pilot Sergeant Thomas Crowe from RAF Llandow was killed when his Spitfire crashed into the side of Ysgyryd Fawr on 8 March 1942. Across the next valley, just below the summit of Garn Wen, a Blenheim, L8610, crashed into the western slope on a training flight from Upwood on 22 September 1940. A memorial listing those who lost their lives, including the pilot, Sergeant Hubert Wilson, the observer and wireless operator, was erected at the site.

Dennis Beavan's father, Roy, originally a draughtsman and designer at Thynns Tiles on Holmer Trading Estate, joined RAF Credenhill's drawing office after a spell filling shells at ROF Rotherwas. His skills came into their own as war ended when he hand-painted this Kennel Club fundraising poster in aid of returning soldiers. *(Dennis Beavan)*

The crash of a twin-engined aircraft on Garron Hill in June 1944, however, had one unexpected consequence. The boy bus conductor Stan Fryer took up the story:

> It was the seventh of June in the afternoon and I heard this plane crash on Garron Hill. The wreckage was spread over about five different hills. I went to see what had happened and at the same time this Mary came from another way. I hadn't seen her before. Anyway, I thought she looked quite good and we arranged to meet. Our first date was a concert in the village hall.

Mary and Stan were married at St Weonards Church in 1950.

15   All at Sea

Despite being a landlocked county, Herefordshire had a close affinity with the Royal and Merchant navies during both world wars. Harold Vaughan, remembered as the mild-mannered ambulance man who served Tupsley's isolation hospital between the wars, had already served as one of the 22 submariners aboard the American-built HMS *H12* in the First World War. In 1914, Joseph Gedge, the son of a former Marden vicar, drowned when the ship on which he was paymaster, HMS *Amphion*, struck a mine. Gedge became the first officer to die in the First World War. The county's seafaring tradition was fostered by an active Naval Cadet Corps and, in one case at least, by a thirst for revenge. Ron Hodges joined the Navy after his older brother lost his life during the 1944 invasion of France. 'George had been killed in Normandy that July and, being a young lad, I [thought]: "I'll get my own back on those Germans."' Ron was posted as a scribe with the Fleet Air Arm, serving with 826 Squadron on the north-eastern coast of Scotland. 'I'd been in the Hereford Sea Cadet Corps so naturally I went into the Navy.'

Seeking revenge: having arrived in Hereford as a London evacuee, Ron Hodges joined the Navy in 1944 after his brother, 22-year-old George Hodges, was killed in the battle for the Pegasus Bridge during the Normandy landings. Ron (*4th from the right on the wing*) served with the Fleet Air Arm in Scotland. (*Ron Hodges*)

A.J. Thomas recalled another mariner, Gordon Williams, the only son of a butcher whose family business was in St Martin's Street, and a fishing friend. Gordon served – and died – as a submariner with the Royal Navy. Thomas also went on to serve in submarines. 'When I entered the service I discovered that our submariner suits were made by Barbour Oilskins. My first cost two guineas.' He had originally worn Barbours during expeditions along the Wye with another fishing friend, Fred Grub who worked for the Electric Company in Widemarsh Street.

One of the stranger (and unsubstantiated) stories of Herefordians travelling abroad on a doomed ship was that involving a consignment of Hereford cattle whose cargo vessel was torpedoed off the Irish coast. Two steers were said to have swum back to the Emerald Isle.

Many Herefordshire men, meanwhile, were serving in the Royal Navy. Arthur Bush of Hafod Road spent five years on the battleship HMS *Nelson*, putting his experiences during Operation Pedestal, an exercise to relieve British forces on Malta in August 1942, into verse:

CONVOY TO MALTA

We were lying at anchor in Scapa Flow
When orders came for us to go:
We sailed on the tide for the mouth of the Clyde
There it was we found our convoy for Malta bound.
We entered the Med at the dead of night
With Gibraltar on our left and Tangier on our right.
Our friends on the Island were in a fix;
Short of food and being hit for six.
Bombs were falling night and day
What a time they had, needless to say.
And action began the very next day
When the carrier Eagle was made to pay.
I saw her go down; I remember the time
It was my birthday – I was twenty-nine.

Bill Jarvis from Hunderton also served on a destroyer, HMS *Zest*. Initially 'sick as a dog' when he went to sea, he was cheered up by his share of prize money – 'I had £9 for helping to sink so many ships' – which he collected at the war's end. 'It was a one-off payment and a lot of money in those days. The Navy kept your prize money records. I didn't refuse it; I went to the post office and drew it.'

Cecil 'Clem' Clements was also destined to become a mariner. The Hereford Co-op delivery boy was a regular at the Odeon cinema and enjoyed watching the *Gaumont British News* pictures: 'You'd see these merchant ships being sunk and the sailors being picked up,' he would recall. The news clips inspired him: 'That got me interested in the

Merchant Navy.' Having a friend in the Merchant Navy had advantages: Colin Jones' family had war workers, mostly munitioneers billeted on them, including a Miss Jones whose mother was postmistress at Staunton-on-Wye. 'We had friends in the Merchant Navy in Fishguard and once a month they sent us a box of fresh fish which we shared with our neighbours.'

Clem was determined to join the Merchant Navy and, knowing that boys of 14 could join provided their parents signed for them, he asked for their support. His mother refused, however, and the boy had to wait until his 17th birthday when he made his own way to Cardiff where he signed on to train as a stoker (since they worked below decks, and in any attack tended to suffer the highest casualty rates, stokers and engineers were in high demand). Clem was given bed and board for 21/- week at a Butte Street seamen's home in the company of a bunch of ex-prisoners, freed on condition they served with the Merchant Navy. Their behaviour caused problems. On one occasion Cardiff police raided the home after a former borstal boy pinched the wax head of Marie Antoinette during a visit to Madame Tussauds waxworks museum. The head had been revealed beneath the lid of the breakfast serving dish that morning.

Now affectionately known by his shipmates as Lofty, Clem set sail on the Island Princess hauling freight around the British coastal ports on what was called the 'rock dodging' route. He was warned of the perils of letting off too much smoke and giving away the boat's presence to the enemy. 'The ships were steam-powered and when the order came down from the bridge, *full ahead* or whatever, you'd be fined 10/- or a £1 if you made too much smoke.'

Clem progressed from stoker to cook, transferring to a Dutch ship run by a German captain who had fought in the last world war, but was now a Dutch citizen, ferrying invasion troops to North Africa. By the time Clem transferred to the Navy's most perilous shipping routes, the Arctic convoys that departed from Loch Ewe delivering high explosives to Russia, he was working full-time in the galley. 'I became second cook and baker. You baked bread every day for about 70 crew and another 20 or so Royal Navy gunners. And you hoped your ship wasn't hit because, if that lot went up, you'd need a parachute not a life jacket.'

Beneath Clem's apparent bravado lay well-founded fears. The Arctic convoys shipped millions of tons of armaments, ammunition and food to Russia to fuel the Soviet offensive against Germany. Lightly-armed merchant ships, protected by Royal Naval ships, struggled under freezing temperatures and German naval and air attacks to reach the Russian port of Archangel and unload their supplies. And despite what he had seen on the *Gaumont British News*, there was little hope of survival for any seaman whose ship was sunk. 'Anybody who said they weren't scared were bloody liars,' he admitted, adding: 'You just got accustomed to it.'

On the outward journey they watched helplessly as neighbouring ships went down – 'We had heavy air attacks and there was submarine activity as well' – and on their

Arctic convoy: Ivan Hall (*right*) with fellow seaman Rogers in the Brazilian port of Santos. Ivan eventually found himself on board the SS *St Clears*, ice-bound in sub-zero temperatures at the Russian seaport of Archangel. When the ice cleared he returned to Britain, the *St Clears* loaded with timber and paper pulp, as part of convoy PQ13. Five of the convoy's ships went down when they ran into a minefield. Ivan's luck held until his ship was attacked and sunk off the North African coast. (*Ivan Hall*)

Lucky survivor: Cecil 'Clem' Clements survived Arctic convoys and being torpedoed off the coast of Dover. In this post-war picture Clem, Joan and the children are enjoying a holiday having ridden to North Wales from Hereford on the family bikes.

return in December 1943 Clem's convoy was ordered to scatter when news reached the captain that the *Kriegsmarine* battleship *Scharnhorst* was heading in for an attack (the *Scharnhorst* was subsequently sunk by the British Navy).

Having run the gauntlet of the Germans, Clem returned home for a spell of leave and encountered a different form of hostility. 'If you didn't wear a uniform people would look at you and wonder why you weren't in the forces.' The seamen's union had resisted government pressure to put their crews in uniform, yet many, including Clem, went and bought one to avoid trouble.

Merchant naval officers were issued with uniforms, although for the 19-year-old deck officer, Ivan Hall, on board the SS *St Clears*, there was no-one to admire it except his ship-mates during the winter of 1942. Ivan, who eventually settled in Ludlow and recorded his memories in *Christmas in Archangel*, set sail on the fifth Arctic convoy, mooring on the dock-side in Archangel to unload their cargo of shells, tanks and crates containing Valentine aircraft. One of Ivan's duties was to record the outside temperature in the ship's log. On New Year's Day 1942 he recorded a record low of minus 40 degrees and the ship became icebound ... for the next six months. The bored crew amused themselves playing home-made board games and, having discovered a music shop in Archangel, forming a scratch band to perform popular songs such as Noel Coward's *London Pride* and Glen Miller's *Chattanooga Choo Choo*.

Eventually, reloaded with a cargo of timber and paper pulp, the ship broke free and returned to Britain as part of convoy PQ13. They passed the ill-fated PQ17 convoy (24 of its 41 ships were sunk) in fog and separated off the coast of Iceland, Ivan's ship reaching the safety of Loch Ewe. The 19 ships in the second half of the convoy hit bad weather, lost their position and ran into a minefield. Five ships went down. 'Yet again I was lucky,' recalled Ivan, whose run of good fortune finally ran out when, working as third mate aboard a Fort class Canadian-built cargo ship, supporting the North Africa campaign, they came under attack. During the first attack, the noise of the assault aircraft and the ship's gun deafened Ivan for the rest of his life. On the second attack the ship was torpedoed: 'We were sunk as simply and as quickly as that. It was sad to see the ship go, but everyone got away safely.'

Clem Clements, meanwhile, had returned to Hereford on leave and met up with Joan Day, a young woman from Hunderton working at ROF Rotherwas as a civilian armaments inspector. 'We'd got married in February that year when he came back from Russia,' recalled Joan. They were not together long: Clem was dispatched to New York aboard the *Mauritania* and put on a train to the west coast where he boarded a new Liberty ship, the *Samwake*. Over 2,000 Liberty cargo vessels were built in record time by American ship builders for the allied war effort, and by July 1944 the *Samwake* was in British waters ferrying troops into France across the English Channel. On 31 July it was attacked by three German *schnellbootes*, torpedo boats.

'We had two torpedoes in us and she was going [down] slowly to start off with,' recalled Clem. 'The captain and some crew went back on board to see if they could salvage her, but she went down.' The sailors calmly took to the lifeboats and were picked up by another ship and taken to Dover. 'We lost the ship's cat and couldn't find the captain's dog – turned out he'd been one of the first into the lifeboats.' The lucky ship's cook returned to Hereford and into the relieved arms of his new wife. 'When he came home on survivor's leave I got pregnant,' remembered Joan. Their first son was born on St George's Day the following April, and by a curious coincidence Clem and Joan's next son and daughter were also each born on St George's Day. They were fortunate their father had survived the war.

16 Wrens and the ATS

Women, too, served in the Navy. The Women's Royal Naval Service, popularly abbreviated to the 'Wrens', had been brought back to life in 1939 having been disbanded in 1919. With the maxim 'Free a man for the Fleet', Wrens were recruited to serve as everything from mechanics and electricians to clerks and range assessors. They were efficient and, with their double-breasted jackets, skirts, shirts and ties, smartly turned out. That, at least, was the opinion of a young Ken

Long lasting: Ken Hursey joined the Fleet Air Arm and was working on aircraft coming off Arctic convoy duties in Londonderry when he met and married Wren Margaret. 'I was only 19 and they said it would never last.' They would be together for the rest of their lives. (*The Hursey family*)

Farmer's daughter: Stella Griffiths, who joined the Auxiliary Territorial Service in Hereford, is seen here smiling for the camera held by ATS friend Mary Millichamp outside the army huts that once stood on Widemarsh Street. (*Rolly Bradstock and Herefordshire Museums*)

Women's work: Kit Gower left her job as a kitchen maid to serve as a regimental policewoman with the ATS. 'When you think about it, it was the women who ran this country during the war; as bus drivers, on trains, in the army, aiming to free men up to go to the war'. (*Kit Hodges*)

Despite the charge of inattention at birth, Iris returned home after three years, and on every Armistice Day afterwards would join the Forces' Parades with no less than five campaign medals pinned proudly to her chest.

Betty Richards from Walford also joined the ATS and was moved to serve with the NAAFI at Ashchurch near Tewkesbury. She was posted to Cyprus, but she had lied about her age (she was 16 when she enlisted) and her manager spotted a birthday card shortly before embarkation that read: 'Happy 17th.' Although her posting was cancelled, the NAAFI kept her on.

Long after the war a group of women who dubbed themselves the 'Old Comrades' met regularly to remember their days in the ATS. Stella Griffiths, Grace Morphew, Marjorie 'Birdie' Bird, Eleanor English, Betty Reihold, Mary Millichamp and Eva Price had joined the ATS and trained at Ripley Barracks, a cold and miserable place according to Stella, near Lancaster. Eleanor served at Garnstone Castle, which had been turned into a nursing home, near Weobley between November 1941 and January 1944.

Kit Gower started training with the ATS in 1942, leaving Hereford for the first time in her life. Kit joined the regimental police at South Wigston, later serving in Leicester and Guildford, leading parades, controlling traffic ('even double-deckers'), escorting prisoners and once disarming a young woman armed with a knife: 'It turned out that the poor kid was suffering because her Mum had just died.'

Kit had some sympathy with the girl. Herself one of 11 children, she'd left Tupsley school and been put in service when her own mum died. She served as a kitchen maid – 'up at five in the morning scrubbing floors until eleven o'clock at night' – but left following a dinner party incident:

> The parlour maid was on holiday so I took the food in and – I know I shouldn't have been listening – but when the lady of the house asked a question, I gave the answer. "Mind your business!" she said, "and get on with your work." I thought: "I'm not having that."

Her life, and status, in the ATS put a spring in her step: 'I'm not being big-headed, but when the commanding officer went past on inspection she'd say: "Perfect." I used to think: "This uniform gets pressed so much it's unbelievable."' Kit was chosen to model the uniform for Swarbrick Studios. They planned a film about the ATS starring Phyllis Calvert and, while the movie was never made, Kit remained proud of her achievements.

17 Prisoners of War

A T HOME, MEANWHILE, WAR SHORTAGES HAD PUT PAID TO THE TANTALIZING aroma of roasting coffee beans ('that unforgettable smell as you walked by,' as Joyce Chamberlain recalled) that usually emanated from Marchant's store in High Town, Hereford. In 1941, however, William and Gertrude Marchant had other worries: their son-in-law, 29-year-old Jack Grisman from Portfield Street, who had married their daughter Marie the year before, was missing. Jack was a flying officer with 109 Squadron based at RAF Boscombe, and his Wellington had failed to return from a special mission over France. Eventually the family learned that the aircraft, piloted by Flying Officer Leslie Bull, had lost power and crashed near Lorient. The crew, including Bull and Grisman, had parachuted to safety, but been captured by the Germans. By 1944 both men were incarcerated in Stalag Luft III prisoner of war camp and planning a mass break-out in what became known as the 'Great Escape'. It would be many years before the family found out the full story of what happened to their son-in-law. After 50 of the escapees, including Jack, were recaptured, they were summarily executed on the direct orders of Adolf Hitler. Two were shot in front of the other prisoners (who, by coincidence, included another Herefordshire airman, Kenneth Smith, who we will meet later).

Families with a father or son held in a European prisoner of war camp could maintain intermittent contact through the Red Cross. One of the sadder services carried out by photographers, such as Doris Townsend at Vivians studio in High Town, was the taking of portraits of family members to be sent through the Red Cross to men being held as prisoners of war.

Doris Kershaw (then Doris Townsend) also remembered how, during the lead-up to D-Day, the photography workers were joined in the studio by RAF personnel processing identity photographs. David Mitchell, a flight lieutenant in Bomber Command, carried his during his Special Duties operation during the invasion. 'My aircraft took off at one minute past midnight on 6 June 1944, and five hours later my crew and I were back at base in East Anglia sipping a large mug of very sweet tea into which had been poured a liberal measure of brandy.' He reflected on 'the stalwarts who were then storming the beaches and who were still fighting and dying.'

Former Bulmers executive Peter Prior, who had been involved in the secret plans for the allied landings, was one of them. He recalled reaching Juno beach 'soaked and seasick' and armed with a .38 pistol. 'This seemed an inadequate weapon for an initial assault' (he was assisting the 3rd Canadian Army to establish themselves) 'but when I reached the beaches I obtained a Bren gun and was ready to sell my life dearly.' Expecting to be met by a hail of bullets, Peter was instead greeted by 'a beautiful 18-year-old French girl who threw rose petals at me and shouted, inappropriately in my case, "*Vive les Canadiens*".' After dark, however, the town where he pitched up, Bernières, was filled with confused firing:

> In desperation, I mounted a loud hailer on my jeep and went round the place shouting in English that people should stop firing. I pointed out that the Germans would not understand what I was saying and therefore, if the firing stopped completely, it would prove that our troops were shooting at each other.

The Normandy landings and the allied advance through France and into Germany lifted the spirits of those still held by the Germans. Mitch Farrington, an RAF navigator, was incarcerated at Stag Luft VI. 'We were betting on when [the allied landings] would happen. On the morning of 6 June, groups had gathered to watch a volleyball match, and the unaccustomed sunshine together with the rumble of gunfire from Russian artillery combined to create a sense of excited optimism.' News finally reached the camp. 'A cheer went up – the invasion had started. A few long-term prisoners were unconvinced – they had heard it all before – but the camp leader produced a translation of the German radio announcement to quell all doubts.' Only then did Mitch discover he had won the camp competition to name-the-invasion-date: 'My prize, an eight-ounce bar of chocolate, was the POW equivalent of winning the pools.'

Jack Hill was also being held by the Germans and had been a prisoner of war for nearly four years when the allies finally crossed into Germany. He and a mixed bunch of other ranks were hurriedly force-marched away from Leipzig where they had been held, to be used as hostages:

> For two weeks we were marched east. However, during the night of 5 May the silence was broken by the news that our guards had fled and we were in no-man's-land. About 40 British prisoners headed towards the American lines some 30 kilometres away.
>
> What a welcome we received when we reached them! A meal of cereals and the news that the war in Europe was to end later that day. The Americans took us to Frankfurt and on to Paris where we were given medical examinations and USA uniforms. Eventually the Americans flew us to Haywards Heath where, again, we were interviewed, received medals and fitted with British uniforms.

Finally put on a troop train to New Street Station in Birmingham, Jack wished his former mates farewell and, on 19 May, headed for Snow Hill Station and the 3.45 p.m. train to Hereford. 'It was my memorable day,' recalled Jack.

Another Herefordshire POW, Ken Williams, was also making his way home. He was hungry. Taken as a prisoner to Germany, Ken, in contravention of the Geneva Convention, had been put to work as a slave labourer in Dresden. For two years he struggled to survive in conditions which he would never forget and which would influence what he chose to do on his return.

'I used to work on the railroad under guard. We had nothing to eat. When you have no food for years you talk [of] food all the time, all day. The fact that we could hardly stand didn't seem to make any difference.' When Ken returned to Hereford he had no doubts about what to do next: 'Being a prisoner of war gave me a big interest in food.' He explained his philosophy to interviewer Sandy Green: 'To get into food you open a café and you're in business. You get into food: it's on the plate, they pay and they're gone.' Ken opened a takeaway in Commercial Street, Hereford, called it Mr Chips and never went hungry again.

Relations between the warring sides were strained when prisoners were being taken. Reg Robins found himself in France after the 1944 allied invasion. Six years earlier the 16-year-old had lied about his age when confronted by recruiting sergeant Bill Pullinger at the Friar Street barracks and still managed to enlist in the army. Now a hardened combatant with the 159th Infantry Brigade, Reg took charge of a group of Germans who had been captured. 'I signed to their officer to hand over his papers, but he spat in my face. I was ready to land one on him,' Reg admitted later. Only the presence of a senior officer held him back (Reg later received the *Legion d'Honeur* for helping to free France).

Back home in Herefordshire attitudes to the growing number of Italian and German prisoners of war often varied. Cyril Ingram lived with his family in Hoarwithy Road, their garden backing on to Bradbury Lines camp: 'There were German prisoners of war there and our Mums used to take them tea and, if we had them, biscuits.' Two of

Captured Germans: Reg Robins, who lied about his age in order to enlist in the army, found himself fighting in northern Europe during the 1944 Allied landings. He had to restrain himself when taking charge of a group of German prisoners. (*Reg Robins*)

Cyril's brothers were in the forces, Ken with the KSLI and Bill on board a Royal Navy escort vessel with the Arctic convoys. Subsequently torpedoed during the war with Japan, Bill Ingram was thrown overboard. 'He was in the sea with two mates, one of whom had lost both his legs. The other man drowned and Bill was rescued, but suffered from TB.' Bill spent the next five years in an isolation hospital at Malvern. Back in Hereford young Cyril, blue-eyed and blond-haired, had started chatting with one of the Germans who spoke good English. 'We heard on the news that we were getting the better of them [the Germans] so, being a bit cocky, I went out and said to him: "Who's best now? Winston Churchill or Adolf Hitler?"

'The German replied: "Oh, it's Adolf Hitler. And when we win the war I'll take you home with me!"

'No, you won't!' replied the outraged lad.

Some children were less critical of their former foes. Fred Klein was a German prisoner of war being held in north Herefordshire. A fellow POW related a conversation he had had with an 11-year-old boy on the farm where he worked. 'He says to the boy: "What you going to be when you're bigger?" And the boy says: "POW".'

People were discouraged from fraternising with the enemy. Griff Loydd, however, recalled residents on Kings Acre Road handing out apples from their orchards to Italian prisoners of war being marched down the road. And the kitchen of the average Herefordshire farmhouse was considerably more accommodating than a gun emplacement on the Front Line as four Italian prisoners, billeted at Aconbury Farm, discovered. According to Henry Moss they were treated almost as part of the family: 'The Italians had their feet under the same table as everyone else,' said Henry. When Sicily fell in 1943, it heralded the collapse of the Italian Fascist leader Benito Mussolini's rule. When word reached the Italians who were working in the fields, recalled Henry, 'they were shouting and clapping.'

Italian prisoners were the first to arrive in Herefordshire. Until the Desert War, which saw the capture of thousands of enemy soldiers, Britain had managed to house its POWs at two camps, one in Cumbria, the second in Lancashire. Now the POWs were encamped across the county. One camp was Wellbrook in Peterchurch near Eva Morgan's family farm, Penlan. Eva recalled the two Italian POWs who lived with them:

> If the camp where they were billeted was a distance from the farm, they could stay with the family: that was popular with the POWs, as farmer's wives, and certainly my mother, were usually good cooks and there was always plenty to eat even with rationing.
>
> Rabbit figured pretty often on the menu (usually alternating with home-cured bacon, most of which was fat) and rabbiting with ferrets was a popular weekend pastime. It was essential too as five rabbits were said to eat as much [grazing grass] as one sheep. And they bred, well, like rabbits!

At nightfall Eva watched the Italians in the kitchen make multicoloured baskets out of wands of split hazel, which they dyed red and green:

> I wonder'd if they used natural dyes? The baskets were oblong-shaped with a solid piece of wood forming the bottom, and upright spars stuck into it and woven in underneath. The sides sloped outwards slightly and there was a carrying handle. They were good and strong and Mum had hers for many years.

The Italians appreciated their bed, board and host and, as a mark of gratitude, presented Eva's mother with a special basket fitted with a lid. She was still using it as her sewing basket 40 years later.

The Wellbrook camp, according to Eva, was purpose-built, with several long huts each covered with corrugated tin and lined with tongue-and-groove boarding. The superintendent had separate, brick-built quarters. 'I remember huts with a curved wall and roof forming a half moon shape where the Italian prisoners made a chapel furnished with chairs and an organ from a disused church at Urishay Castle.'

Some Italian POWs were based in a camp at the South Hereford Hunt Kennels near Wormelow. Later they were housed at Bryngwyn, according to Eileen Lloyd who lived at Wormelow during the war. Initially, a company of Indian soldiers (possibly Rhajputs assembling for the anticipated D-Day landings) was based here: 'The men slept in small round tents and Bryngwyn Park was provided with concrete standings and large marquees to accommodate them and their magnificent horses. They also had a pack of mules, which were used to collect provisions from Tram Inn Station.' The sound of the mules on the move along the Dewchurch Road sent the children running to meet them: 'The Indian soldiers were very friendly and colourful: they'd hoist us onto the already loaded backs of the mules.' After the Indian soldiers left to take over Holmer School, presumably before departing for Europe, Bryngwyn served the New Zealand Forestry Corps, working in Mynde Wood, ('their cookhouse was by our Granny Thomas' fence and we'd be treated to iced buns and sweets'). Bryngwyn later housed German POWs.

Three Italian POWs worked at Hill Farm in Llanwarne, according to Chris Tomlinson who recalled the mysterious case of the disappearing eggs:

> We had run very short of eggs although there were plenty of chickens. Suspicion fell on the Italians, but the farmer, Mr Spode, did not say anything to them. Instead he went round their coats, which were hanging in the barn, and clapped his hands either side of their pockets, breaking the eggs.

Relations with the Italians improved somewhat when they were invited into the farmhouse to make spaghetti. Chris, however, was unimpressed: 'It seemed to me, as a six-year-old, a very messy business.'

Egg mystery: Young Maureen Beauchamp (*above*) with Italian prisoners of war whose camp was based at the South Hereford Hunt Kennels in Wormelow. The arrival of several POWs at Mr Spode's farm in Llanwarne (*left*) coincided with a sudden drop in egg production. (*Maureen Beauchamp, Derek Foxton, Christopher Tomlinson*)

Later in the war a German prisoner of war arrived to work at Hill Farm. 'He was very nice: he told me he did not want to fight and had surrendered as soon as the opportunity arose,' recalled Chris.

Wellbrook in Peterchurch was also now housing German POWs. One, Otto Carl – 'tall, handsome and always smiling' – remembered Eva Morgan, came to work at Penllan farm. Otto was joined by his friend, Emil Franz, and the two learned to plough and plant, to reap and mow with Eva's father's green Standard Fordson tractor. Otto earned a special place in her parent's affection by saving Eva's two-year-old sister Mary from a terrible accident. She had been playing in the yard as her father drove the cart-horses towards their stable. 'The huge horses galloped round the corner into the farm-yard as Otto was washing his hands at the outside tap. Seeing Mary playing right in their path he vaulted the four-and-a-half-foot high wall and scooped her up.'

Eventually Otto and Emil were moved to the camp at Tupsley where Otto, previously an atheist, converted to Christianity. The two men returned to Germany, Otto to the west, Emil to the east. Nothing was heard from Emil again, although Otto wrote regularly to Eva's mother, Margaret. More than 65 years after the war he revisited Penlan, 'still tall, dark, handsome and smiling,' recalled Eva. 'Otto was pleased to see that the hedge he had pleached, at the bottom of the Castle Pitch, was still growing well and kept trim.'

Not all POWs wanted to come back when the war had finished. Henry Moss remembered one gifted German mechanic who wanted to stay in Herefordshire until he received news from home: 'With tears in his eyes he told us: "They have found my mother. I must return."'

Hans, one of three German POWs working at Ufton Court farm near Holme Lacy, was a favourite in the Perkins family. He was trusted to supervise their daughter Elizabeth's riding lessons. Hans had lost contact with his own family, a son called Heinz and his wife Hilda, during the war. When hostilities ceased Jeanne paid £23 to the Red Cross to try and trace Hans' family. 'Hilda was found in Berlin, living on nettles and sparrows, having been imprisoned in a concentration camp,' recalled Elizabeth. Two of Hans' POW workmates at the farm, Max and Otto returned to Germany, while Hilda and Heinz were brought to England to be reunited with Hans. Although they settled in Herefordshire for the rest of their lives, Hilda never recovered emotionally from the horrors she had experienced at the hands of the Nazis.

Elizabeth Glover remembered a succession of Italian and German POWs who worked on farms at Holme Lacy, Dinedor and Belmont, and who, like Hans, remained in England. Belmont Abbey, in particular, gave support and sanctuary to several former POWs who chose to stay in Herefordshire, putting up in dilapidated caravans and eking out a living with casual farm work. War had ruined their lives.

Life saver: Emil Franz (*top*) and Otto Carl (*middle*) standing beside the Morgans' Standard Fordson; and Otto Carl pictured in 1946 (*bottom*). The two German POWs stayed at a camp in Peterchurch working at Penllan, the Morgans' farm. (*Eve Morgan*)

Close friends: German prisoners of war in a Herefordshire hop yard, thought to be Pomona Farm at Bartestree. Many close relationships developed between local people and POWs. (*Herefordshire Lore/ In Our Age*)

Others who stayed made a success of their new lives. Guenter Matthes, a former member of the Luftwaffe ended up in a prisoner of war camp at Weston under Penyard. Eventually he worked as a ghillie on the Wye for Sir Thomas Pearson: the two men had been on opposite sides at the Battle of El Alamein. Manfred Klein – Fred to his British friends – had experienced a brief, but dangerous war before he found himself passing through a succession of Herefordshire POW camps including Ledbury, Tupsley, Brimfield and Ullingswick.

Fred had survived one of the most punishing sieges in history, the 900-day blockade of Russia's Leningrad (the old city of St Petersburg) by Finnish and German forces. Three Klein brothers, Fred, Hans and Andreas, the sons of a cowman from Transylvania, had fought side by side. By the time the siege came to be lifted in January 1944, Hans and Andreas were both dead.

Fred served in the 3rd Tank Regiment, dressed in three coats against the intense cold and driving a MAN munition truck ('It was so cold you had to keep it running all night'). At one point he found himself 70 kilometres behind the attacking Russian lines where, briefly, he joined the bodyguard of the notorious Waffen SS General Felix Steiner's unit (after the war Steiner would campaign for the rehabilitation of his disgraced fellow SS soldiers). As the Russians closed in, Steiner was flown out, his bodyguard left to the mercy of the Soviets. But there was no mercy:

> We were spotted by a Russian. He shouts: "Everybody run!" and they just held a machine gun on the German soldiers and the [Germans] fell like flies. There was no question of taking prisoners. Fred and a friend hid in a ditch. "Shall we shoot each other?" asked my friend? And I said: "Not yet."

Eventually a party of 17 Germans escaped, and after hiding in a wood made their way into a small village under the cover of darkness. When Fred spotted five Russian helmets lined up on the veranda of a house the men once again took to the ditches. Moments later a Russian guard came past. He was seized and stabbed and the men fled. They finally reached the port of Riga where they boarded the last German ship to leave – 'the ship next to us was hit by artillery and I saw people drowning. I had nightmares over that. Long, long time.'

The group, now reduced to five, reached Berlin just as the Russians moved in on the city. Fred carried a small Luger pistol in his jackboot – 'I intended to shoot myself if the Russians take me' – while he searched desperately for an American to whom he could surrender. There was a confused exchange with the first GI he met. The infantryman struck him with his rifle: 'I thought bloody hell, he was going to shoot us.' On 8 May he finally found a company of GIs, surrendered and was put in a prison camp with 20,000 others. There was nothing to eat. When two soldiers called for a volunteer, Fred stepped forward and found himself making U.S. beds. 'The Americans were very untidy.' One GI took a liking to Fred, loaning him his shaving razor and giving him his unfinished meal. Then the prisoners were rounded up and driven to a nearby wood: 'It dawned on me they [were going to] bloody shoot us, you know?' (the Germans had summarily executed civilians and combatants alike, especially on the Eastern Front). 'But they lined us all up and [told us to] pick up all the litter!'

Fred was eventually handed over to the British. Shuttled between Ullingswick, Ledbury and Brimfield, Fred ended up at the Brickfields camp in Tupsley where, in his shabby POW uniform marked with a diamond-shaped yellow star, he picked apples for a Fownhope farmer and looked after cattle for a Captain McIllroy. 'I said to him: "Look, I don't know whether you say *Mr, Squire, Sir, Your Highness* and all this?" And you know what he said? "I'm a gentleman." I never forget that: "I'm a gentleman".'

Fred had one more 'gentleman' to encounter: champion pedigree Hereford breeder Captain de Quincey of The Vern, Marden:

We were sent to work to the Vern and we were by the house and the Captain comes up and says: "You're new aren't you?" I says: "Yes."

"How would you like to work here?"

I said: "Well we got to go back to where we were for few days." But he took my number – we all had numbers, didn't we? And my number is 13. Unlucky 13.

Quincey was true to his word. He arranged for Fred to join the Vern and help with the pedigree herd of Hereford cattle. Eventually Fred became the herd manager. Some years later Captain de Quincey did Fred another favour, offering his German manager a pair of maiden heifers of his choice. Later in his life Fred reflected on his decision: 'I picked all right because one of the maiden heifers picked was Klein Atlantic and the other was Klein Baron. Which sold for twelve thousand quid.' It was enough money for the former POW to buy his family home near Pembridge.

Post war: Hereford celebrates Battle of Britain day in September 1948. By now several German and Italian prisoners of war had chosen to remain and make Herefordshire their home. (*Derek Foxton*)

18 Subterfuge and Deception

I T WAS DIFFICULT DURING THE WAR TO GAUGE WHAT WAS HAPPENING. LETTERS FROM the war zones, and the national and local press, were so heavily censored that people came to rely on word-of-mouth for their news. Lord Haw Haw, or William Joyce the Nazi stooge who broadcast to Britain under his signature call sign 'Germany Calling', offered his own version of the news. Chillingly, Joyce informed his Herefordshire audience about the bombing of Rotherwas (although he also claimed the railway station had been hit) when the local press referred only to an incident at a factory in the West Country. But when Lord Haw Haw declared that starving Herefordians were reduced to eating foxes it was too much for Gordon and Phyllis Parker, licensees of the Tram Inn at Eardisley. They launched their own ceremonial fox pie at the Tram, a rich meat pie crowned with a stuffed fox's head (its true contents remained a secret to all those outside Phyllis' kitchen).

Yet someone in Herefordshire *was* assisting the Nazis, if inadvertently, as evidenced by the disturbing experiences of pilot navigator Ken Smith. Ken, whose father ran a pub in Cotterell Street (possibly the Britannia) was in the RAF, flying with 78 Bomber Squadron over Schweinfurt in February 1944, when his Halifax was hit. This was Ken's 22nd operation – one for each of his years – and he flew, as always, with a couple of photos of his wife Norma Beavan taped to the wall in front of him (he also carried a good luck keepsake of Norma's inside his flying jacket: one of her bras). Norma's photos carried a message, written in Russian, explaining that he was a British pilot – falling into allied Soviet hands carried its own risks.

As their plane faltered, Ken and the rest of the crew bailed out, to be picked up, not by Russians, but by a German Home Guard unit. Only their rear gunner was lost (although he had apparently parachuted out safely he was never seen again). After being paraded in front of hostile villagers, Ken was taken to the notorious prison camp Stalag Luft III, scene of the 'Great Escape' and the execution of Jack Grisman. But before his imprisonment Ken was subjected to interrogation. He told the *Hereford Times* in an interview: 'I was interrogated and would only give my name, number and rank.' He was taken aback when the German interrogator revealed that they not only

Glad to be back: former POW Squadron Leader Ken Smith (*back, right*) with friends Roy Beavan (*front*) and Captain Derek George (*left*), surveying a flooded St Martins Street, Hereford in 1947. (*Dennis Beavan*)

knew, correctly, that he had been born in Hereford, but that his wife, Norma, worked for Leone's, a hairdresser in High Town. German intelligence, which was really interested in the latest British navigation aids, had gleaned the information from their copy of the *Hereford Times*, regularly delivered to Nazi headquarters through a neutral country. Ken, unlike Jack Grisman, survived his incarceration, but he was left wondering who had regularly dispatched the *Hereford Times* abroad.

Everyone undertaking war work signed the Official Secrets Act. They included Wilfred Bowen, chief worktaker at ROF Rotherwas, whose team of 100 fellow worktakers calculated the weekly incentive bonuses of the factory's 2,000 workers. Wilf was careful to say nothing about his work to friends or family (a whisper went round the factory that he had been appointed chief 'undertaker'), but he was aware of persistent rumours of sabotage at Rotherwas: 'There were one or two surprise discharges [of personnel]. The tale used to go round: "They've sacked so-and-so; I wonder what he's been up to?" Things were very secretive.'

Sisters Betty and Florence (Sally) Griffiths lived on the Rotherwas estate next door to the factory's chief accountant, Mr Broaden. While Sally worked in the offices issuing travel vouchers to those living in the country, Betty was recruited by Mr Broaden to sort Christmas telegrams in London. 'I remember cables for the royal family, but you couldn't read them: they were all in code. You couldn't read anything.' The same culture of secrecy operated within ROF Rotherwas: 'It was all hush-hush. Everything was kept very quiet.'

Prisoners of war: 22-year-old Bombardier John Oswald interviews captured Germans. Fluent in French, German and Italian, he had been transferred to the Combined Services Detailed Intelligence Corps (CSDIC) after being overheard chatting with villagers during his time with the British Expeditionary Force as they withdrew from France in 1942. 'One of our officers said: "You speak French? Can you order the wine for our officers' mess?"' Instead Oswald was moved to CSDIC and trained in interrogation techniques by the renowned Colonel Alexander Scotland. 'We were taught to be kind; hectoring the Germans was no use.' Later, screening POWs at Wolfsberg in Austria, John Oswald exposed a seemingly ordinary Obergefreiter (senior lance corporal) as a senior SS officer wanted for war crimes in Yugoslavia. The officer was handed over to the authorities, tried and executed. (*John Oswald*)

Occasionally the official news channels got things wrong. Two Hunderton boys, Geoff 'Mutt' Cole and James Jones, were best friends at St Martin's School. Both joined the Parachute Regiment and both were embroiled, along with other British and Polish forces, in the battle to secure Holland's strategic bridge at Arnhem in the autumn of 1944. At one point Mutt swam across the *Neder Rijn*, the Dutch section of the Rhine (he attributed his swimming skills to 'good training in the Wye') before being pinned down in a gun battle with Germans near the bridge. James Jones was already dead, killed by a stray bullet from a loaded rifle that had been accidentally dropped in the road (he was said to have been the first of the 1,500 Allied Airborne Unit casualties at Arnhem). In the confusion that followed, however, Mutt's parents were told: 'Your son has been killed in action at Arnhem.' It wasn't until Mutt returned on leave and discovered his parents in mourning that the true story came out.

The wartime work of some individuals would remain a mystery long after the conflict was over. In December 1941, with the nation still short of military personnel, the government brought in the National Service Act, calling up all unmarried women aged between 20 and 30. Jeanne Perkins, the 22-year-old farmer's daughter from Ufton Court farm at Holme Lacy noted the new Act in a letter to a friend. Having just given up running the milk bar in Commercial Street to take charge of the canteens at ROF Rotherwas, she wondered what the future held for women like herself:

> I see they are expecting, before Christmas, to introduce a new National Service Act for every man and woman in the country. It may seem strange at first for some of us, but I'm all for going for it if it means a speedy end to this dashed war.

Then, in around 1943 Jeanne was moved from managing the canteens to driving lorries loaded with explosives. 'I will be sorry to leave the canteens, because as you know I'm all for feeding men's tummies,' she wrote to a friend, and soon found herself involved in highly secret and highly dangerous work.

Jeanne and another woman began driving lorries on unspecified missions to Glascoed, a munitions factory in South Wales, and Blockley (possibly the Northwick Park camp used by the Americans and later occupied by German POWs). Jeanne's daughter Liz Glover believes the young women carried high explosives: 'They were presumably carrying high explosives because they weren't allowed to stop; they were instructed to fix any mechanical problems that arose themselves; and they had to vary their routes and the times of their departures.'

Contrary to military rules, Jeanne kept a tiny diary noting not only her pay and hours ('3 January 1943, 11.5 hours' and 'ROF wages £4.0s 5p') but a number of secret and inexplicable car journeys: 'Drove to ???, dropped off …' Was she delivering or collecting secret agents or spies?

By now Jeanne had met, and was soon to marry, Hereford vet John Ryan. Ryan, working at the practice in Ryelands Street, was himself leading a double-life as a member of Churchill's secret army. Jeanne and he were married in 1943 and Jean later told her daughter light-heartedly that she would never want her husband to lose his temper because 'he had been trained to kill.'

A Hereford landowner who was recruited into what was almost certainly the same clandestine unit, but who adamantly refused to be identified even 70 years later, recalled the day of his own enrolment: 'The telephone went one evening and the voice said: "Would you care to volunteer for something?" I ended up in a thing called 202 GHQ.' Covert Auxiliary Units had been set up by the Prime Minister in the summer of 1940.

'Churchill realised we had lost everything in Flanders,' recalled the gentleman farmer. 'There were chaps getting back with no equipment, and if Jerry came we'd got nothing. And Churchill wanted a unit that would serve, not under official command, but as irregulars. It was absolutely secret.' He met the next man in the chain of command: 'I only knew the first one [in] the link: our man Todd had served behind the lines.' Captain John Todd, according to Bernard Lowry and Mick Wilks (in *The Mercian Maquis*) was a former stockbroker from Llanvihangel Crucorney, and the first intelligence and recruiting officer for Herefordshire and Worcestershire.

Todd's reputation for bloodthirsty fighting talk was confirmed by this recruit:

> He said: "No matter what you think, Jerry will find out [intelligence] from you. He will torture you and probably only one in a hundred will be able to [avoid confessing]".
>
> The farmer described their unit, one of four or five in the county, as being in a wood some distance away, dug out by engineers and you could walk along, but you wouldn't know it was there.

That was our base for equipment, and the idea was that we might operate for about a week [after a German invasion]. Then we'd be caught. The aim was to get information about what was going on and disrupt Jerry, [and] to actually, if possible, kill any officer where we were dumped. We were to lay low until Jerry was in your area, then try and pick off the important individuals and kill them. Some of us were sent away to a special training school and had a very interesting course in unarmed combat and how to be pretty bloody nasty.

When the threat of a German invasion had subsided, the Auxiliary Units continued to function:

We were kept going quietly. Churchill was always a cautious man wasn't he? I don't know the reasoning, but everything was kept under cover and then some of us, we were sent down on D-Day to the Isle of Wight. I suppose the idea was we'd been taught to use a knife and a revolver and it was quite extraordinary how defenceless the average man is when it comes to "nasty" fighting.

After D-Day this individual stepped down. 'When the invasion was thought to be a success, and there was no way that Hitler could mount an invasion, that was it.' The farmer, like the vet John Ryan, was in a reserved occupation: 'I concentrated on food production,' concluded the landowner.

Like Jeanne Perkins, several women were involved in cloak-and-dagger work. The most famous was Violette Szabo, the 23-year-old British agent tortured then murdered at Ravensbrück concentration camp in February 1945. Violette stayed with her English cousins at Wormelow before the war and again while she recuperated between missions to France to work with the Resistance movement.

There were others. Peter Holman, a schoolboy in Kington during the war, liked nothing better than playing with friends:

War, at first, made little impact on the lives of me and my friends, Neville Ovens, Raymond Parker, Terry Creamor and John Stimpson. We drove flocks of sheep to market, caught minnows in the Arrow and watched Flying Fleas, small one-man operated airplanes in khaki drab, trundle along a field on the edge of town carrying, we thought, mail to the American Camp. Once, a low-loader pulled onto Yeoman's depot laden with the fuselage of a large military aircraft still with bandoliers of ammunition inside. We clambered through it, unchallenged, whilst the driver had a break.

Since his friend John Stimpson was the nephew of Arthur Dickinson, proprietor of the Bridge Street Picture House, the boys were regularly allowed into the projection room. The downside was lunch with John's French mother, Blanche, who sometimes served boiled nettle tops: 'I was convinced I'd get stung.' Blanche led a double-life. Like Violette Szabo she was parachuted into occupied France to work with the Resistance movement, while husband Ray, a well-known local artist, served in the army. Blanche was rumoured to have kept in touch with her sister by a radio transmitter at the Dickinson household.

On a more prosaic note, A.R. Willis of Three Elms Road, Hereford recalled having to be careful with his camera. With the traditional May Fair banned from High Town in the interests of national security, the Showman's Guild erected a single, brightly coloured stall outside Bell's tobacconists to fulfil the conditions of the Guild's charter allowing the Fair to be held continuously. 'I wanted to photograph it, but there were always civil and military police on duty and it was dangerous to take photographs in public as one could be arrested on suspicion of being a spy.'

The war drove individuals like Szabo and Stimpson into performing acts of extreme bravery. However, one group which received little recognition for the courage of their convictions were the conscientious objectors.

19 Conscientious Objectors
by Dr Elinor Kelly

I T IS SOMETIMES FORGOTTEN HOW GREAT WAS THE REVULSION AGAINST THE HORRORS of the First World War. There was a widespread urge to join the peace movement that developed, led by organisations such as the Fellowship of Reconciliation, the No More War Movement and the Peace Pledge Union. When conscription was reintroduced in 1939, the Prime Minister himself spoke about the lessons learned and the need to respect conscientious objectors:

> We all recognise that there are people who have perfectly genuine and very deep-seated scruples on the subject of military service (…) We learned something about this in the Great War (…) it was both a useless and an exasperating waste of time and effort to force such people to act in a manner which was contrary to their principles.

Many men did indeed resist military service. Over the next six years of war, as legislation expanded the net of conscription, a total of 60,000 men and 1,000 women applied for exemption from armed service. Of these, 18,000 were refused, 39,000 were either allowed exemption conditional on doing alternative civilian work, or put on the military service register as non-combatants. Only 3,000 were given unconditional exemption. About a third appealed against the decisions; subsequent appeal tribunals revised about half of these after re-examination.

For the men of Herefordshire, the first step in resistance to war was to register in the local Employment Exchange and then to attend a hearing of the Conscientious Objector Tribunal in Birmingham, led by Judge Longson. He presided over 6,233 cases: 1,119 were refused registration and became liable for military service, 980 were allocated to Non-Combatant Military Service and required to enlist. 4,035 were allowed to return to work. Only 89 were allowed full exemption.

The first Herefordshire men to reach the Tribunal in 1940 met with a varied response. Three men were removed from the register of COs. Leonard Sayers of 16 Ledbury Road,

Hereford, a former soldier, was refused because the Tribunal did not accept his new pacifism; A.C. Riches of 111 Grandstand Road, Hereford was told that he must subject himself to Army medical examination to test the medical unfitness he claimed; and Robert Popkin Shaw of Garway House, Garway was removed from the register of COs because he had made no effort to find Non-Combatant work.

John Merlin Thomas of Hadon, Whitehorse Street, Hereford was confirmed as a CO until he completed his college studies. J.C. Carmichael of Bromley Cottages, Hoarwithy was confirmed as a CO after he explained he had lost his former job when he registered as an objector. The remainder – Ernest Pugh of 1 New Cottage, Stretton Sugwas; and Hereford men Charles Cyril Henry Smart of 14 Canonmoor Street; Albert Willetts of 19 Widemarsh Street; Percy Hughes, of 29 Westfaling Street; Stanley Finch of 3 Westfield Street; W.H. Meadham of the Adult School in King Street and E.M.C. Blundell of Myrtle Villas, Prior Street were allowed Conditional Exemption, requiring them to remain in their current jobs. E.W. Malcolmson, a medical practitioner in Staunton-on-Wye, was not allowed to join the Royal Army Medical Corps, but told to return to work.

Three men opted to serve in the Friends Ambulance Unit: Raymond J. Birkett of Oakengates, Hergest Road, Kington; Paul F. Croft, 35 Hampton Dene Road, Hereford; and Howell W.P.J. Jones of Compton House, Hay-on-Wye.

Almeley farmers R.T. Davies, John Jenkins and Basil Hobby, all sons of First World War COs, were told to stay in their current work. Basil became liable for conscription in 1942 when he reached the age of 17. Even though he was the son of a First World War CO and member of Almeley Wootton Quaker Meeting, he emphasised how difficult it was to hold to his principles:

> I was 15 when the war broke out and my older friends went off to war. I had to register for war at 17 and, as a Conscientious Objector, had to appear before the Midlands Tribunal in front of a judge. It was an intimidating experience: I had to state my reasons for not wanting to fight. The Friends Ambulance Unit had enough recruits, but there was a shortage of food with ration books. I was asked if I agreed with the killing of animals and answered yes, but only if they were humanely killed. I was then asked if I was prepared to go to prison, but I felt that it was better to provide food. My father, James, hadn't gone to war in the First World War. It was hard to be a CO when others had gone to war and I felt embarrassed. Some of my school friends didn't want to go to war but had to, and some of them were killed and never came home. My wife's brother was at D-Day and survived but suffered psychologically.

Meanwhile, Herefordshire County Council was debating the matter of how to ease tensions about the COs in their employment. It was agreed that all members of staff who were conscientious objectors would be offered continued employment only on the basis of the pay of a private soldier, with the alternative of taking leave without pay for the duration of the war. Hereford City Council debated a harder line, wanting to

Conscientious objection: Clement Attlee meets Hereford's munitions workers at Rotherwas in July 1941 (Imperial War Museum). Attlee, a Labour member on the War Cabinet, was also a veteran from the First World War having fought alongside many Herefordshire soldiers at Gallipoli. His brother Tom, however, had refused to fight and was imprisoned for his conscientious objection on religious grounds. (copyright © The Imperial War Museum)

ensure no COs were appointed to the staff of Council schools and current staff should be ordered to take leave of absence. They were reminded that the Government had made repeated statements that COs should not be penalised, so it was accepted that existing CO staff should be retained.

Two men who had a very difficult time were Aubrey Bufton of Leominster who refused to undergo the mandatory medical examination and became liable to imprisonment; and J. Moorwood of Ross-on-Wye, who was imprisoned in Gloucester in December 1941 for refusing his medical. Also, three men who accepted enlistment in the Herefordshire Non-Combatant Unit. L. Jacob, Gilbert Lane and Ernest Thompson were named in a House of Lords debate about how badly the military were treating COs.

Friends' House: built in 1672 and meeting place of the Almeley Wootton Quakers – including Almeley farmers R.T. Davies, John Jenkins and Basil Hobby. Basil, the son of a First World War Conscientious Objector, was forced to explain himself before a judge at the Midlands Tribunal: 'It was hard to be a CO when others had gone to war, and I felt embarrassed.' (*Andy Johnson*)

20   Foxley Camp

As victory in Europe and the Far East approached, there were furtive comings and goings in the woods near Mansel Lacy: squatters were discreetly moving in to any empty huts they could find at the former U.S. military camp of Foxley. The trespassers were homeless servicemen and their families desperate to find a roof over their heads after fighting for their country.

Foxley Camp stood in a woodland clearing on the Davenport estate. The first group of buildings had been put up by Canadians. They were followed first by German prisoners of war and then the American Army hospital. Eva Morgan, like many young Herefordians, noted the arrival of these foreigners with interest:

> After the Italians, the Germans arrived and after them came the Poles who helped with the haymaking. The Poles didn't live with us [at Peterchurch], but several married local girls and made their home on farms in Herefordshire. Many Poles had been in the Russian gulags or slave camps. Others escaped from [German-occupied] Europe and fought with the Allies. They couldn't go back to Poland, now in Soviet-occupied Europe.

Charlie Evans, the son of Mansel Lacy postmaster Ernie Evans, watched the arrivals:

> There were Polish army here to start with then the [Polish] women came. The queue for the post office used to run down the road as they waited with their parcels. They were buying so much stuff to send back to Poland that the Post Office sent a special van to come out and fetch the parcels.

The land they occupied, Foxley, was an historic house and garden established by one of the leading lights of the eighteenth-century Picturesque Movement, Uvedale Price. Sold to the Davenport family (descendants of the famous china manufacturers), the estate had seen better days, and in 1948 the house itself was demolished. The camp, however, now housed a thriving community of Herefordshire families with nowhere else to live, and Polish expatriates under Captain William Hawker, a veteran of the First World War who was in charge of the Resettlement Corps. Many families would retain fond memories of camp life, with its cinema, gym, Catholic church and school. Pat Davies' first teaching job was at 'little Poland' in 1959 when she was placed in charge of 25 five- to six-year-olds. 'Mrs Letitia Kurhan, the head teacher, had built the school up from the beginning and took pride in doing her best for the school,' remembered Pat. 'There were Christmas shopping trips to Hereford and summer bus trips to Barry Island.' Vera Bond also taught at Foxley School in converted army huts which were:

> very cold in winter; boiling in summer. The children were well-brought up and obedient. And it amazed me how an infant would start school knowing no English, but, by the end of term, could speak quite well. We did have a few mistakes such as one boy accusing another: "He's telling liars."

One Herefordshire woman who met her future husband, an American GI, there remembered the camp with fondness: 'I have lots of happy memories of the camp, riding my bicycle there from Westhide, 15 miles away.' Another regular visitor was June Williams, whose friend's sister married a Polish soldier and went to live at Foxley. 'We discovered a tower and on the walls were hundreds of addresses of Americans who had spent time there.' The girls wrote to some and were delighted when they received the occasional letter back.

The building stone for Foxley Camp came from a quarry on Shucknall Hill, and was worked by Indian soldiers, according to Basil Morgan. One Shucknall Hill resident was surprised to find one of the Indians inside her house. 'He wasn't trespassing; he was simply curious to see the inside of an English home,' reported Basil. When the camp was dismantled, nothing, including the Shucknall stone, went to waste. Phyllis Edwards related how her aunt built her home in Yorkley in the Forest of Dean from Foxley's beams, bricks and stone, while villagers at Edwin Ralph relocated a complete U.S. hospital unit to their village where it served as the village hall for Edwyn Ralph, Collington and Thornbury for 50 years.

Foxley Camp: the base at Mansel Lacy served as a German POW camp and a U.S. army hospital, but under Captain William Hawker (*above*) it provided homes for families who had lost their homes in Poland, and Herefordshire people returning from the fighting. Hawker, who had already served in the First World War, was appointed officer in charge of the Polish Resettlement Corps. (*Wendy Cummins*)

Some years after the camp had been dismantled, Hereford builder Charlie Bloxham sent a group of bricklayers, including one of Foxley's former Polish residents, to construct new pillars for gates at the King George V Playing Fields. The Polish man was Eddie Dzierza. The other men referred to him only as 'that fucking Pole.'

'I told them: "My name is Eddie. If you want something, call my name." But they were joking and I lost my temper.' Eddie struck one man with his shovel just as Charlie Bloxham returned to see how the work was progressing. 'I was thinking: "That's the last day with Charlie Bloxham."' But Charlie told Eddie: 'No, you stay. They got the sack.'

It was a bitter victory for a man who had been forced into slave labour, been injured fighting for the Allies and who had buried his mother with his bare hands when she died of hunger.

Eddie's fellow builders had no idea of the journeys undertaken by Polish people who were now calling Herefordshire their home. And Eddie only revealed his own story many, many years later.

Polish survivor: Eddie Dzierza survived slave labour in Siberia, starvation in Kazakhstan and being badly wounded fighting with the Polish Army in Italy. He made Hereford his home after a spell at Foxley Camp with his young family. (*Stasia Dzierza*)

The Germans had invaded Poland from the west in 1939; the Russians, after Stalin made a pact with Hitler, from the east five days later. Eddie was 14 when the Russians arrived at his family's farm. His father, Yann, rushed off to join the Free Polish Army while Eddie, his mother Eugenia, and his five brothers and sister fled their village with a pair of horses. They stumbled into a battle between heavily-armed Soviet forces and a group of Polish cavalrymen on horseback, who, with swords drawn, attacked the Russians. The family witnessed the slaughter of the Poles as one of their own horses was killed and Eddie's sister narrowly escaped being hit by a stray bullet. Joining the refugees fleeing the Russians, Eddie then got into trouble with a party of Ukrainian soldiers. He had found a small eagle statue, the symbol of Poland, lying in the street and waved it at the soldiers, shouting angrily: 'One day this bird will fly over you!' He was spared summary execution by the intervention of a Russian colonel, passing on his horse. 'Let him go,' he told the Ukrainians. 'One day he'll be a good man.'

The family found sanctuary with another Polish family, but it proved a temporary respite. In December the Russians were back: 'They gave my Mum 20 minutes to pack everything.' The family was herded onto a cattle truck and for the next 22 days they and hundreds of other Polish families were transported across northern Europe into Siberia.

'When we arrived, there was a big snow. It was very cold. The Russian soldiers told us: "You must march. If anybody falls out they will be shot."' Chillingly, they were true to their word: 'A lot of mothers were carrying everything and eventually they fell and collapsed to the right or left. They were bayonetted or shot.'

The family were housed in wooden huts in a concentration camp built by German POWs and surrounded by forest. Yet there were no watchtowers or high fences: 'You can't escape – the nearest station was 100 kilometres away.' The 14-year-old was sent to work in the forest with a chisel and a hammer to mark trees for grading. He was glad of the work: 'If you work you have a portion of bread and, if you got brothers and sisters, then you must share. If you don't work, you don't have the bread'. Sometimes Eddie and his brother stayed working in the forest, miles from the camp. They encountered bears and learned to stand still until the bear went away. One time the horse bringing their supplies was attacked by a bear. Their horse fought back, kicking and pawing the bear, but it was badly mauled and died later.

Eddie's oldest brother, Tadush, fell ill with meningitis. 'We'd got a good doctor, but he had no medicine because everything – food, bread – was going to the Russian army.' Tadush died.

When Germany attacked the Soviet Union in June 1941, Stalin ordered the release of his Polish prisoners. 'We were still in the camp. Everybody was meeting and singing the Polish national anthem and then we got the news we were free. That same day everybody got a special document, like a Russian bus pass! The commander came and told us: "You must leave."'

The Polish General Wladyslaw Anders had announced plans to form a Polish army, but as Soviet-Polish relations deteriorated (Stalin had his eye on the former Polish territories) 71,000 Polish people were evacuated from Russia in 41 train-loads and 25 shiploads, mostly down through the Middle East. Eddie, his mother and her four other children were loaded on to railway cattle trucks, and for over three weeks made their way down to Tashkent in Kazakhstan:

> The five of us travelled from Siberia to Kazakhstan. My only wish now was to get a nice loaf of bread, eat it and die in a corner. In Kazakhstan the people were Muslim. We were begging. Sometimes you got a piece of bread, sometimes nothing. We stayed in a little house of clay and straw, and now my youngest brother and sister went very sick. They went to hospital and they both died.

Eddie had gone to visit them and now had a 70-kilometre walk back across a desert to his Mum and his two remaining siblings. He fell asleep in the desert and awoke to what seemed like a mirage: 'There was a cow eating straw. I milked her into my mouth! I was thinking: that was a miracle!'

When Eddie reached home, Eugenia, his mother, was dying of starvation. 'When you touched her, she shouted. It must have been painful.' She died three days later and

Eddie, scraping out a shallow grave with his hands, buried her. The 15-year-old walked his surviving brother and sister into the town:

> I was thinking that for me the Polish Army is better because I would get food. Next day I found some Polish people. I put my brother and sister into an orphanage' (they would survive the war and make their way to England).
>
> One man gave me new trousers and a new shirt. I started a fire, put my shirt on top to burn off the fleas, and then walked to the station for a train to Busork to join the army.
>
> When I was on my way, there was this gang stealing things. I am a Pole, but I got a Russian passport, and when the KGB came for the gang they took me to their station for a couple of hours, questioning me and hitting, you know. I got the punishment yet I hadn't stolen anything. I said: "I am going to Busork for the Polish Army". And then they let me go.
>
> When I arrived I had to go to the army doctor. He ask me: "How old you are?" I put three years on my age. And he looks to me. I look to him straight to the eye, you know? And he checked me and he said: "You all right."
>
> The Polish Army was now fighting in Tobruk. I trained on signals and Morse Code. Then I got malaria. When I get out of hospital I was sent to Egypt and the Canal Suez. I was Polish Cavalry with armoured tanks. We fought in Italy, at Monte Cassino where nearly 5,000 of our soldiers died.

Hit in the head by shrapnel, Eddie was flown to India for an operation. He received a second shrapnel wound later. Then, in a field near Ancona, he was strafed by gunfire from German planes:

> My friend got a rifle and I got the ammunition. He went from me and I said to him: "Stop! Don't go." He didn't listen to me. He got a couple of bullets right through and he was dead. I take his identity tag, break the line: put one ring with the number on in the mouth and one ring in the pocket. Then when I stood I feel I something very warm.'

Eddie had been shot five times in the stomach. 'I put my belly in my army cape and I start walking, but I collapse and an Italian woman come and I ask her first which part I am: German or English. She say: "Inglaterra". And she went and got the ambulance.'

Again Eddie survived and, on the eve of victory, he found himself in Bologna. The summer heat was so strong he and his two comrades stepped out of their armoured car for a moment. Both friends were hit and killed by sniper fire.

As the VE celebrations started, Eddie passed the mutilated bodies of the Italian leader, Mussolini, and his mistress. Passing Italians were spitting on the corpses.

'Everybody went in the street, you know, drinking, lot of flowers, lots of kisses.'

Later, at a former camp for Jews, now a transit camp for Polish people, Eddie met his future wife, Emilia. But they faced a new problem: where to go. His homeland was under East German rule; Poles who had been forcibly returned had been murdered. And the Italians were unfriendly, 'because a lot of Mussolini people don't like Poles. When you talk they notice.'

In the end Eddie and his family settled for England, and eventually Foxley Camp. Many years later Eddie went for a job as a bricklayer at Credenhill, now an army base. He recognized the foreman as the man he had attacked over his racist remarks. Eddie turned to leave, but the man called after him. 'He called me: "Eddie, come back." I went. And he gave me the job.'

Camp life: (*above left*) Charlie Evans, who had witnessed the Camp being built, revisiting the site nearly 60 years later. (*Herefordshire Lore/ In Our Age*). (*Above right*) children at play at Foxley. Many buildings were erected during the war by the McAlpine 'Flying Squad', the labourers arriving in double-decker buses, which served as transport, canteen and sleeping quarters. Foxley impacted on the lives of many Herefordshire people: Dylis Price, for example, met a U.S. pilot recuperating from his wounds at Foxley, at the May Fair. They married and when he was sent back to the States she followed: 'I'd never been further than Malvern – I was only 17!' Having forged her father's signature to secure the right papers she sailed for the States on board the *Queen Mary*. Foxley was demolished in 1961/ 62. (*The Derek Evans Archive*)

21 Victory

Eddie Dzierza and his remaining family members, held in transit camps, had little opportunity to celebrate the European victory when it came. Others, however, did – both on 8 May, Victory Europe (VE) Day, and 15 August, Victory Japan (VJ) Day.

Barbara Philips (later Barbara Sharpe) from Ross was boarding at Hereford Training College. She and her pals had already spent a morning of cancelled lectures scraping blackout paper and netting off College windows when, on 1 May, Miss Jennings announced that, with VE Day approaching, the students should make arrangements

Party time: VE Day coincided with Mary Lewis' 20th birthday. Mary (*second right*) from Leeds, was on her way to the pictures when she was 'kidnapped' by a local publican. Corporal Harold King (*third right*) from Lower Bullingham was on leave from RAF Pershore and heading across High Town when he was also approached by the landlord: 'He already had the others and he wanted an airman to complete his party. "There will be a drink in it for you," he promised.' The group went on to help with the Berrington Street party for around 100 children. Afterwards the drinks were on the house. 'We helped serve teas and probably had a couple of ciders, but there my memory ends,' said Mary. (*Herefordshire Lore/ In Our Age*)

Going bananas: Londoner Joy Davey recalled 'we didn't see bananas at all [during the war]. Mother would buy parsnips and cook them and mash them and put banana essence in and make banana sandwich! Well, it tasted like bananas to me!' Bananas were on every table at this Berrington Street party (*above*). Street party in Church Street Hereford (*below*). (*Herefordshire Lore/ In Our Age*)

for taking two days holiday. 'On May 4 there was a news flash at 8.40 p.m.,' she recorded in her diary. 'The German troops in north and west Germany, Denmark and Holland have all offered to surrender tomorrow at eight. In town everyone was buying Union Jacks and red, white and blue things. All the shops were decorated with flags. The railways are going to run on VE day so we'll be able to get home.'

The May Fair was at last back in Hereford and Barbara dashed round with two mates. 'My luck was in. I won two glasses and a toy dog on Rolling the Balls.'

Barbara caught the train back to Ross. It was not yet VE Day, yet the Market Hall was already flood-lit and hung with flags and the town centre was packed. 'There were hordes of people, mostly drunk – especially the soldiers. They were all singing and dancing and letting off fireworks. Some chaps then proceeded to ring the fire bell – this went off for ages. The police didn't attempt to stop anything!'

The next morning Barbara boarded the 8:15 bus back to College in Hereford, disappointed to be missing the dancing and bonfire planned for Ross that night. In the event, with 'terrific crowds in High Town', the student teachers at the College had a bonfire of their own and a generous evening out extension until 10.45 p.m. 'We sang and roasted potatoes till about 11 o'clock and ended up with the College song.' The next day the principal, Miss Jennings, planted a commemorative cedar tree on New Land, opposite the College. 'She said we could bring our grandchildren to see the tree when it had grown.'

Still a young lad and living with his family next to the almshouses at Coningsby Hospital, Richard Smith was given some pocket money and told to go shopping: 'Mum sent me and my brother to Haines to buy a flag each to wave in High Town.'

The landlord and landlady of the Lichfield Vaults, Titch and Ethel Rowberry, contributed to the Church Street party. The crowd included Molly and George Coleman, Dickie Mailes, the local barber and his family, the shoe repairer and his family, a tailor from East Street, Colin Geddes and Nanny Powell from Leicester Place – together with a large photo of Winston Churchill. Throughout the war Titch sent cigarettes to two customers, taken prisoners of war in Germany, via the Red Cross. When the pair returned, Titch tried in vain to stop them drinking away the pay that had accrued during their incarceration. The pub hosted a welcome home party at the 'Lich', and while Royal Naval sailor Bill Jarvis was there he was thinking ahead:

Lichfield Vaults: landlord Titch Rowberry behind the bar in the 1960s. During the war he sent cigarettes to two former customers who were then prisoners of war in Germany. (*Tim Rowberry*)

VJ Day: It's Victory Japan Day, 1945 and the band of 124 (Hereford City) Squadron of the Air Training Corps pass through High Town with, among others, Alan Willis on tenor drum, Bobby Griffiths, Drum Major Goodwin, Cpl Drummer Derek Cross, and Reg Colwell. (*Alan Willis*)

The main thing then was to find a job. You were given a pinstripe suit and a trilby hat I never wore – looked like you came from the workhouse! You had a gratuity, then, so much. And you had your one-off payment of prize money, what [shipping] you sunk.

For now the partying went on. A bandstand had been set up in the middle of High Town on VE Day, and after speeches and marches the partying began. Jean Muldowney was on Castle Green with:

Glen Miller music, *In the Mood* and *Little Brown Jug*, blaring out from the band-stand. I joined a snake of people of all ages doing the conga which wended its way into High Town where the City was alive with celebrations. The atmosphere was magical. I was home late that night, but I didn't get into trouble because everyone was singing and dancing. The war was over.

Margo Morris, then a staff nurse at the County Hospital, had been allowed by her ward sister to head into town for an hour's celebration on VE night. Accompanied by other nurses and some convalescent soldiers, she made her way to High Town where, even though it was one o'clock in the morning, people were still celebrating.

Beryl Sadler from St James had been working at ROF Rotherwas' pay station through VE Day. By the evening, as she told her friend Penny Jones, she was ready to party. 'I made my own shoes with a high, wooden wedge heel to which I nailed strips of red, white and blue webbing. They were a picture!' Proudly, she sallied forth with her brother, home on leave from the RAF. But when the shoes disintegrated, leaving Beryl walking on a bed of nails, she threw them away. 'I had to get my brother to piggy-back me home. So much for designer shoes.'

March past: Hereford Air Training Corps, led by Squadron Leader Gordon Lamputt behind the band in a victory march through High Town in 1945. (*Gordon Lamputt*)

Royal Naval man Jim Lawes was in London. 'I can recall the sheer relief. Everyone came out in the streets; every pub was drunk dry. There was music, laughter, dancing and lights. The blackout was over and house- and street lights glowed at last.' He lost his sailor's hat as he was caught up in a conga that danced down the Mall to Buckingham Palace: 'Shouts for the royal family.' His companion, a young ATS woman, threw hers to the crowd. 'After escorting her to the underground station I finished up about 4.00 a.m. stretched out on a platform at Waterloo Station.'

Prinia Prior, who would eventually move to Sutton St Nicholas with husband Peter, was an Aircraft Direction Wren at the Royal Air Force Station at Yeovilton in Somerset:

> Following some suitable congratulatory prayers at Divisions, the Captain announced that all flying was cancelled for the day and it was to be a general holiday. Another Wren and I decided on the spot that Bournemouth had a good

deal going for it and we set out in blazing sunshine to hitch-hike there, snacking en route off oranges and ice creams.

The town's fountain was decorated with coloured lights, and festive crowds were milling around on the promenades and beaches. Much to our gratification, we were quickly picked up by two really glamorous Canadian Air Force officers who took us to dinner at the Queens Club and later to a dance in their mess.

Afterwards, with hundreds of others, we spent the whole night in games and revelry on the beach – respectable games, I suspect, for we two Wrens were only 19 and these were days of innocence. Some people slept on beach chairs, for it was a mild and starry night. Everyone was in a state of happiness, sometimes natural, sometimes induced, marred for us only by the need to return to Yeovilton and to duty at dawn.

Beach party: on a mild and starry night, 19-year-old Wren Prinia Prior and her friend spent the night playing 'respectable games' on Bournemouth sands. 'Everyone was in a state of happiness', she recalled. (*Martin Prior*)

Stan Keeble, who served in the RAF from 1942 to 1947, was even further from his Herefordshire home in southern Italy:

> After VE Day I was able to take more advantage of my whereabouts and sample the delights of my surroundings, which included weekly visits to the opera in Naples, trips to Sorrento, hitch-hiking to Rome and visiting the ruins of Pompeii. But the only trip we were all waiting for was the trip home.

The VJ Day celebrations were a little more sober, although Margo Morris's airman husband Bill went to Cambridge, along with his fellow air crew, heading for their favourite pub, the Baron of Beef. It was already packed when they arrived. 'Listen lads,' shouted the landlord, 'the drinks are on me. Serve yourselves'.

Barbara Philips was in Wisbech on a National Union of Students farm camp picking apples. 'There was dancing in the streets and the bridge was lit with coloured lights.'

Hereford student teacher Gladys Pugh and her friends in the Student Christian Movement had celebrated VE Day by cycling to Symonds Yat 'in glorious sunshine' and returned to tuck into a VE Day cake, baked by the kitchen staff and decorated with petals from red geraniums and blue geum.

On VJ Day, however, they were attending a Christian conference at the Boys' School in Cheltenham, the cheery atmosphere chilled by the news that the atom bomb had been dropped on Japan. 'Great arguments about the rights and wrongs were discussed, but people of our age were involved in the armed forces. Whatever their views the war was shortened by this event.'

Still at war: Howard Laws, later vicar of Aston Ingham and Lea, was in India when VE Day was being celebrated at home. (*Peggy Laws*)

Don Cornford, who had been looking death in the face after being captured by the Japanese, was less circumspect about the bombing. He had been lying wounded in a military hospital after the sinking of his ship HMS *Repulse* on 10 December, 1941. When the Japanese overran the island he was taken prisoner, first in Changi jail and then at the Selerang barracks. He was put to work on the Burma Railway and buried many of his mates who died from disease and starvation. Don weighed around five-and-a-half stone when a Guards Regiment officer called Captain Redman parachuted into the Bangkok prison camp where he was then being held. 'The war is over,' Redman told Don.

Vi Thomas, a Lancashire lass who made Herefordshire her home, remembered the VE and VJ celebrations:

> For our VE Day party neighbours brought out the dried egg and homemade jam to make cakes; paste pots and spam tins were emptied; the local farmer gave us extra eggs. Someone produced jellies she had hoarded for years; another some solid icing sugar to decorate the sponges. Several women went and queued for pork pies. We pooled all our cheese rations and another produced several jars of pickled onions – we didn't ask their age!

Turban and gloves: at least one woman (*centre*) remembered her gloves when she joined families greeting Field Marshall Montgomery on a visit to Bradbury Lines in 1953. Also in Royden Willetts' photo were Betty Barton from Blakemere with her daughter Christine and friend Roger Hesten with hat and glasses (*right*). (*Royden Willetts*)

Kitchen tables were brought out, covered with cloths and adorned with union jacks and vases of flowers and laid down the street. After tea and children's games the evening's entertainment began.

> Old Mrs Hanks suggested the men push her piano from her front room onto the road for a sing-song. My husband George and three others started to move it, forgetting her path was on a slope. The piano careered straight through her gates, but she didn't care: "My man will fix that when he gets home. He'll soon be back." We sang and danced and then lit a bonfire. What a fire! Sheds had been emptied to fuel the blaze and the firemen were called when it ran out of hand.
>
> But George's older brother Bill was a prisoner of war in Japanese hands and we couldn't forget the war still raging in the Far East. When VJ Day finally came my husband and I went to Clydach, Abergavenny to celebrate with his parents. The mountain was ablaze with bonfires, everyone forming great circles, singing and dancing, but George's father refused to celebrate. He was still waiting for news of Bill. It wasn't until some weeks later that we learned Bill had died of *beri beri* the day after VJ Day.

In the late 1980s Vi helped found the county reminiscence group Herefordshire Lore with friends Roy Kennett, Alf Evans, Vi Woolaway and Jim Thomas. Later she reflected on those halcyon, early post-war years as Herefordshire came to terms with peace. She and husband George had arrived in Hereford looking for work. Once George found a job at Rotherwas the couple moved to Foxley.

> When you came out of the forces, you filled in a form to go to wherever you intended living for peace time. We had the option of going to Foxley until we got a proper house. It wasn't very convenient: George used to cycle seven miles in the morning and seven miles home at night. And he wasn't alone in doing so. But we had a house of our own and we made the most of it. You had two bedrooms, a living room and a kitchen. The condensation was bad and they didn't have proper windows, but George found some on a building site and put them in. He did me a porch too and we were cosy.
>
> My children went to Mansel Lacy school. One time the dog went missing and when I went to pick up my daughter Kate she said, "Mummy, we've had a visitor." The dog had been to the school and they'd kept him there, in the dolls house, all morning.

Two years later, in 1954, the family was allocated a house on the new Newton Farm estate.

> Mother and father were already at one of [Hunderton's] ministry houses, paying about 25 shillings a week. Money wasn't very high, but it was adequate. Some things were still rationed and I knew one or two people in that particular time who only had potatoes for their main meal. But we always managed a dinner; the children were always tidy and we didn't live it up with smoke and drink and cars. It was just our home. That was all it was with us.
>
> George used to take me to the cinema and he'd go to football every Saturday afternoon. Then I'd get the children dressed and go up and meet him. We'd have a mooch round Woollies [Woolworths] and on Sundays we always went to Castle Green with the children and then round to the duck pond. I loved Hereford. It was clean and beautiful.
>
> I do remember one morning when my mother said: "Come on, we'll go to town." I got ready to go and then she said: "Where are your gloves? You don't walk around Hereford without your gloves. You're not in Lancashire now."

REFERENCES AND FURTHER READING

Beattie, Derek, *The Home Front in Ludlow during the Second World War*,
   Logaston Press, 2010.
   — *South Shropshire's First World War*, Logaston Press, 2014.
Davey, Eddie (ed.), *The Oral History of the Parish of Marden 1900 to 2007*, Marden
   History Society, 2008.
Dinedor Heritage Group, *Dinedor and Rotherwas Explored*, Logaston Press, 2014.
Edmonds, John, *The History of Rotherwas Munitions Factory, Hereford*,
   Logaston Press, 2004.
Hall, Ivan, *Christmas in Archangel*, Trafford Publishing, 2009.
Herefordshire Federation of Women's Institutes, *Herefordshire Within Living
   Memory*, Countryside Books, 1993.
Hughes, Philip, *Wings over the Wye*, Philip Hughes, 1984.
Johnson, Andy and Shoesmith, Ron (eds.), *The Story of Hereford*,
   Logaston Press, 2016.
Jones, Marion, *Proud to be a Timber Girl*, 2013.
Laws, Bill (ed.), *Amazing How Times Change*, Hereford City Council, 1992.
   — *Herefordshire's Home Front in the First World War*, Logaston Press, 2016.
   — (ed.), *In the Munitions*, Logaston Press, 2003.
Lowry, Bernard and Wilks, Mick, *The Mercian Maquis*, Logaston Press, 2002.
Lowry, Bernard, *The Shropshire Home Guard*, Logaston Press, 2010.
Macklin, Fiona, *The Story of RAF Madley*, Logaston Press, 2006.
Oswald, Captain John, *A Kitbag of Memories*, 2011.
Pollard, John, *No County to Compare*, Lapridge Productions, 1994.
Power, Maria (Lita), *Beyond the SS Habana – A Family Story*, (privately published).
Shoesmith, Ron and Barrett, Roger, *The Pubs of Leominster, Kington and North West
   Herefordshire*, Logaston Press, 2000.
Stokes, Tom, *A Life's Journey*, Owl Books, 1994.
Wilks, Mick, *Chronicles of the Worcestershire Home Guard*, Logaston Press, 2014.
Williams, Dennis and Mintram-Mason, Sue, *Into the Storm – The Making of a
   Bomber Crew*, Mintram Williams Books, 1998.
Wood, Gordon, *Railways of Hereford*, Kidderminster Railway Museum/
   Gordon Wood, 2003.

Baxendale, James, on Randolph Trafford: www.ewyaslacy.org.uk
Herefordshire Archive and Records Centre (HARC): www.herefordshire.gov.uk/archives
Herefordshire Family History: www.herefordshirefhs.org.uk
Herefordshire History: www.herefordshirehistory.org.uk
Herefordshire Libraries: www.herefordshire.gov.uk/libraries
Herefordshire Light Infantry Museum: www.herefordshirelightinfantrymuseum.com
Herefordshire Museum Service: www.herefordshire.gov.uk/museums
Shropshire Regimental Museum: www.shropshireregimentalmuseum.co.uk
The Worcestershire Regiment: www.worcestershireregiment.com

GENERAL INDEX

INDEX OF PEOPLE

Also from Logaston Press (www.logastonpress.co.uk)

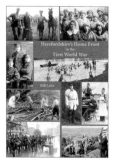

Herefordshire's Home Front in the First World War
Bill Laws
176 pages, 242 × 171 mm
b&w illustrations
ISBN: 978-1-910839-06-5
Paperback, £10.00

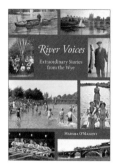

River Voices: Extraordinary Stories from the Wye
Marsha O'Mahony
256 pages, 242 × 171 mm
b&w illustrations
ISBN: 978-1-910839-31-7
Paperback, £10.00

In the Munitions: Women at War in Herefordshire
Herefordshire Lore
128 pages, 171 × 242 mm
b&w illustrations
ISBN: 978-1-873827-98-7
Paperback, £10.00

The History of Rotherwas Munitions Factory, Hereford
John Edmonds
128 pages, 171 × 242 mm
b&w illustrations
ISBN: 978-1-904396-27-7
Paperback, £10.00

The Story of RAF Madley
Fiona Macklin
88 pages, 171 × 242 mm
b&w illustrations
ISBN: 978-1-904396-65-9
Paperback, £6.00